The Complete Vending Machine Fundamentals

Volumes 1 & 2 In One Book

by

Steven Woodbine

Copyright Notice

Copyright © Pratzen Publishing 2007. All rights reserved. None of the materials in this publication may be used, reproduced or transmitted, in whole or in part, in any form or by any means, electronic or mechanical, including photocopying, recording or the use of any information storage and retrieval system, without permission in writing from the publisher. To request such permission and for further inquiries, contact:

Pratzen Publishing, 512 NE 81st Street, Ste. F #171, Vancouver, WA 98665

First Edition: 2007

ISBN 978-1463508685

Trademark Disclaimer

Product names, logos, brands, URLs, web site links, and other trademarks featured or referred to within this publication or within any supplemental or related materials are the property of their respective trademark holders. These trademark holders are not affiliated with the author or publisher and the trademark holders do not sponsor or endorse our materials.

Copyright Acknowledgement

Photographs attributed to a third party are the property of such third party and are used here by permission. All such attributed photographs are subject to the copyright claims of each respective owner.

Legal Disclaimer

This publication provides information about the vending machine industry and includes references to certain legal and accounting principles. Although the author and the publisher believe that the included information is accurate and useful, nothing contained in this publication can be considered professional advice on any legal or accounting matter. You must consult a licensed attorney or accountant if you want professional advice that is appropriate to your particular situation.

Warning Labels and Safety Procedures

Certain vending machine manufacturers now recommend that a Warning Label be affixed on certain vending machines to warn of the danger involved in tipping, shaking, or rocking the vending machine. State and local ordinances may require similar labels or other safety-related labeling or procedures depending on the product sold and the design of the vending machine. Some photographs in this publication may show vending machines which are not equipped with the recommended warning labels or other required safety equipment. Prior to purchasing, installing or using a vending machine or any associated equipment or materials, the user must comply with all applicable laws, regulations and safety procedures.

"The Best Only Gets In The Way Of Good Enough"

-Russian Proverb

Table of Contents

Vending Machine Fundamentals Volume 1   7

Chapter 1: Understanding Your Goals and Expectations   11

Chapter 2: Funding Your New Business   17

Chapter 3: Business Structures   33

Chapter 4: Business Preliminaries and Risk Management   43

Chapter 5: Types of Vending Operations   55

Chapter 6: Service Vehicles   77

Chapter 7: Finding Locations   87

Chapter 8: Setting Up and Keeping Locations   103

Chapter 9: Moving Your Machines Around   109

Chapter 10: Servicing Your Machines   119

Chapter 11: Inventory Management   129

Chapter 12: Protecting and Maintaining Your Machines   141

Chapter 13: Record Keeping, Business Analysis, and Tax Planning   155

Chapter 14: Putting It All Together In a Business Plan   167

Vending Machine Fundamentals Volume 2   177

Chapter 1: Getting Started With Bulk Vending   181

Chapter 2: Bulk Vending Machines & Equipment   197

Chapter 3: Bulk Vending Products   215

Chapter 4: Bulk Vending Inventory Management   235

Chapter 5: Finding Locations & Installation   251

Chapter 6: Servicing A Bulk Route   265

Vending Machine Fundamentals

How To Build Your Own Route
by
Steven Woodbine

Preface

Thank you so much for purchasing this book! You have taken your first step to starting your own vending machine business. The vending machine industry is a cash-driven industry that generates billions of dollars in annual sales. While there are many large companies that participate in this industry, there are many small operators as well. Many vending machine businesses consist of nothing more than independent owners, who personally service their own machines. This is one of the best parts about the vending machine industry. You have the ability to grow your business to the size most appropriate to you. If you only want a few machines you can stop there, however, with hard work, perseverance, and business savvy there is no reason you cannot grow your little company into one of the big boys.

This book is intended for anyone who wants to be their own boss, earn extra income, or start their own business. Maybe you have seen a line of people in summertime itching to feed their money into a soda machine. You might want an investment that is not tied to the stock market. It could be that you have always dreamed of starting a small business after retirement. There are any number reasons that you might be interested in vending machines and this book will help you get started. You do not need an MBA to understand the ideas in this book. Many of the ideas are very easy to understand and those that are not are accompanied by helpful examples, pictures and figures.

That being said, it must be stated that the contents of this book are my personal perspective and opinions on the vending industry. Others in the vending industry may have points of view that are completely contradictory to the ones contained in these pages. I do not profess in anyway to be an authority on any of the subjects contained herein. For accurate and complete information on all aspects of business management always seek professional advice.

-Steven Woodbine

1

Understanding Your Goals and Expectations

Before you begin to build a vending machine company you should consider what it is that you wish to accomplish with vending machines. You should also take time to consider how a vending machine route will fit into your life.

There are different types of vending machines and there are many options that can be used to build a business that is best suited to your needs, time, particular skills, financial needs and your profit goals.

The best way to begin understanding and clarifying your goals is to ask yourself many questions. From the answers to these questions you can learn what you want in a vending business and where is a reasonable place to start. Equipped with this information before specific issues are discussed in this book, you will be able to pick out particular bits of information that are especially relevant to you and your plans.

Questions to Ask Yourself About Your Goals

"What do you want to achieve with a vending machine business?"

At this point you do not need to know how you will achieve your goal. This will be discussed in detail in later chapters. You most likely already have an idea of why you are interested in vending machines, but it is a good idea to specifically identify it.

- Do you wish to gain financial independence?
- Do you want to earn a little extra money?
- Are you trying to pay tuition for your children?
- Are you looking for a weekend business?
- Are you looking to save a little extra money?

- Are you looking for an investment outside of the stock market?
- Are you looking for the tax benefits of a small business?
- Do you need to supplement your retirement income?
- Do you want to be your own boss?
- Do you want to spend more time with your family or friends?
- Do you want more time to continue school?

"Why are you interested in a vending machine business?"

It would be a good idea to identify what it is about the vending machine business that interests you. You may have heard something about the industry before. You may know someone who works with vending machines. It would be a good idea to figure out what it is that interests you in particular.

- Are you interested in being your own boss?
- Does the idea of writing your own schedule intrigue you?
- Do you like working independently?
- Do you enjoy working with machines?
- Do you like the idea of owning your own business?
- Would you benefit from the tax aspects of owning a small business?
- Are you intrigued by investing in yourself?

"How will a vending machine business fit into your lifestyle?"

This is an important question. When beginning a small business many people will underestimate the demands it can put on them or overestimate their available time. A vending machine business can be designed for just about any lifestyle but you need to accurately understand the way you live and what time resources you can provide. You also need to understand what your lifestyle will require from a vending machine business.

- Will a vending machine business be your only job?
- How many days a week can you provide to a vending machine business?
- Does this business need to support you financially?

- What responsibilities do you have to your family?
- Do you like to take long unplanned vacations?
- Are you willing to work mornings, nights and weekends?
- How many days a week are you willing to spend servicing machines?
- What activities do you participate in that you are committed to?
- Are you a student?
- Do you already have job requirements?
- Are you retired?

"What skills to do you posses that will be an asset to this business?"

This question is not designed to point out that you are inadequate to start a vending machine business. Far from it, this question is designed to highlight areas where you might be more comfortable hiring others to help or areas that you need to focus on and grow as a business person. An insufficiency in any of these areas can generally be overcome without much difficulty.

If you are not a strong person, you can hire people to move your machines. If you do not like talking on the phone, direct mail ad campaigns may be best for you. If you are not mechanically inclined, hire a repair technician. You can see how problems like these can be solved. Many solutions are addressed in this book. However, highlighting your particular skills early on can help you decide what type of vending business will best play up your skill set and which type of vending business models you will be most comfortable with.

- Are you an organized person?
- Do you like to work with numbers?
- Are you physically strong?
- Are you mechanically inclined?
- Are you a good problem solver?
- Are you comfortable in a car for extended periods?
- Do you like working with people?
- Are you comfortable talking on the phone?
- Are you a good writer?
- Are you comfortable working as a salesperson?

- Do you have any relevant experience?

"What are your financial resources?"

A bulk vending machine can be purchased and filled for as little as $50. With that fact in mind, just about anyone can afford to start and grow a vending machine business. Briefly considering your financial resources (more specific analysis of your financial situation will be carried out in a later chapter) will give you an idea of the resources you can use to grow your business.

- About how much money do you have saved?
- How much equity do you have?
- What is your annual income?
- Do you have a pension?
- Are you living on a fixed income?
- What are your monthly expenses?
- Do you have retirement savings such as an IRA?
- Do you pay a mortgage?
- Do you make car payments?
- Do you have enough money to buy everything that you need right away? Will you need financing?
- Will you need to buy equipment slowly over time?
- Do you have enough money to see yourself through low sales or rough patches?
- Can you leave yourself a satisfactory financial cushion if your business is unsuccessful?

Once you have sat down and honestly considered these questions and any others that you might find relevant, you can begin to methodically build the business plan that is the goal of this book. Remember to be honest with yourself, if you do not provide correct or honest answers to these questions, you can construct an unrealistic plan with goals that are beyond your reach or inappropriate to your lifestyle.

2

Funding Your New Business

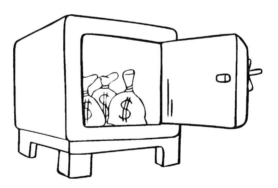

Before you build a house you must lay the foundation and even before that you must do some planning. An ounce of prevention is worth a pound of cure – better to plan well first.

Before placing even a single machine, you need to decide many things such as the form that your business will take, where to get the money to pay for your equipment, what your business will be called and what to do with the money you make. Chapters 2, 3 and 4 of this book deal with many things that should be taken care of before you even consider placing a machine. Pay attention to these pages. Little mistakes made during the early life of your business can become big headaches later.

Money and Financing

Any business venture is going to require money. There are two big questions that need to be answered. The first of these questions is "How much money is it going to take?". The second question that must be addressed is "Where am I going to get the money from?". Let's take them in turn.

How much money is this going to take?

The simple answer to this question is as much or as little as you want to invest. It is certainly possible to go out and buy a single used bulk vending machine for $50. You could find a location through someone you know that doesn't require a commission or sign up bonus for free. That's it! Before you know it you have what could be called a vending business and you are out a mere $50 in capital investment. Now that is probably not what the majority of people who read this book are hoping to start. Most people are interested in large vending machines in high volume locations that make lots of money.

Here is an example to consider that illustrates potential start up costs. Let's say that you are interested in setting up a vending location at "ABC Incorporated". "ABC Incorporated" has 50 employees. The manager of this business says that they would like both a full size snack machine and a full size soda machine (machine types and specifications will be discussed in detail in a later chapter). This is a newer business and the machines are, at times going to be seen by customers and investors. No commission is to be paid to the location.

So here is what you are going to need in terms of machines. You are going to need newer, more professional-looking snack and soda machines. For the snack machine a minimum of 24 selections would be recommended and a minimum of 8 selections for the soda machine. The machines will need to take dollar bills as well (this increases the cost of the machines and will be discussed later as well).

Presuming that you are going to buy the machines yourself (later, how to get machines without large capital investments on your part will be discussed), you are probably going to need to spend $800 for each used machine and $2000 for each new machine. That is a total cost of $1600 to $4000 per location. This may seem like a large sum of money, but the return on investment will warrant it. Let's look at that in detail.

As was already stated, ABC Incorporated has 50 employees. For the purposes of this discussion assume that you go and get the new machines for $2000 each. So far you have spent $4000. Right off the bat you can begin to depreciate you machines. That is an immediate $571 dollar tax write off each year for the next seven years. How this number is computed, and what it means will be discussed in a later section. In addition, you are going to be making sales at this location. Figuring conservatively, estimate that a quarter of the employees will buy something from your machines each day. The item they are buying costs $1. That is $12.50 each day. That is $62.50 each week. That works out to $3250 per year. Subtract the cost of product from this total. This amount is usually 50% or so. That leaves a gross profit of $1625. Divide the gross profit by the amount you spent on the machines and you come out with a number slightly larger than 40%. Many investors would be very happy with a profit of 40%.

Now the financial aspects of this example account have been discussed, consider that it took you maybe 1 hour a week to service this account. That's all! Take your $1625 gross profit and divide it by the 52 hours you put into it and you get $31.25 per hour. That is what you are getting paid for one hour of your time. Remember the best part-you are working for you! You don't have to ask to take a break or start 5 minutes late. You are in charge.

Now the scenario we looked at is just a model account. Obviously, accounts can do better and accounts can do worse. Businesses in an industrial setting where things are greasy and grimy care less about machine appearance. This means that you can get away with older less expensive machines. Some accounts will only accept brand new machines. There are lots of variables. The important thing to keep in mind is that these variables can be managed to create a very profitable return on investment and increased financial independence in your life.

In addition, depending on the amount of money you want to invest and your particular point in life, you can find a vending business that is appropriate for you. If you have $2000 dollars and you only want to service routes once a month, a bulk candy route would be perfect for you. Remember, you control how much you spend and invest.

Where am I going to get the money?

Starting a new business is a process that needs all the attention of entrepreneur. Borrowing large sums of money can be a complicated and frustrating experience. If not done carefully, large borrowing can be risky as well. There are many considerations that need to be looked after. You must consider all types of financing, including terms and interest rates. In the end, the decision is yours and you must live with your decisions. Do your homework and proceed carefully. Before considering any financing options the first thing you should do is take stock of your financial situation. You need to know what your strengths and weaknesses are, before talking to any lenders.

Credit Rating

Regardless of which business form you ultimately choose, you will most likely have to make some sort of a personal guarantee to obtain financing. Few lenders will be enthusiastic about lending to a brand new business. Your inexperience in this business will be seen as a risk and will require collateral to secure a loan.

The first thing that you will need to do is obtain and properly interpret your credit report and rating. Your credit rating is simply a numerical score based on your credit report, as computed by a credit reporting agency. In the United States there are three major credit reporting agencies. These agencies, in no particular order, are TransUnion (www.transunion.com), Equifax (www.equifax.com) and Experian (www.experian.com). Current federal law (2007) allows you to request, free of charge, a copy of your credit report from each of these three agencies once a year. To obtain your actual credit score there is usually a small fee. This fee is well worth paying.

Once you get your credit ratings you will need to interpret them. You can do this online to get an idea of where you stand, or you can take your credit report and score and speak with a lending professional. Obviously, the higher your credit rating, the lower your interest rate will be and the easier it will be to find financing.

Examine Your Equity, Income and Expenses

For term loans (loans that are of a fixed duration and payment schedule) lenders often look at your total monthly income when they consider your application. They are not very often impressed by projected sales but instead want to see that you will have the ability to make the loan payments regardless of how the business develops. The lender will analyze your net worth, check on your savings and determine any equity that you have to borrow against.

An important factor when considering a loan application is the net worth of the individual or corporation. The net worth of an entity is everything that the person or corporation owns minus any outstanding debts. These debts include unpaid money on mortgages and other loans, government liens, judgments etc. Make sure to include such things as brokerage accounts and money in the bank. For the sake of simplicity omit money that is tied up in any tax deferred accounts like IRAs or 401(k) s. These types of accounts can be used to finance businesses but doing so is far more complicated.

If you are interested in this option, search for information on self-directed IRAs online. A great deal of information is available and there are many investment companies out there willing to help.

Equity is the value of an item that you own (such as a house or car) that is free from any claim. An example will help to make this point clear.

Paul bought a house 5 years ago for $100,000. His mortgage was 100% of the value of the home and totaled $100,000 at that time. At the point of purchase Paul had $0 in equity in the house. Since then Paul has managed to pay off $25,000 of his mortgage. At this point his house is still worth $100,000 (for the sake of simplicity) and his mortgage is now $75,000. The difference ($100,000 - $75,000) between the value of his home and the money he owes for the home is $25,000. This is his equity. Paul can state he has $25,000 in equity in the house to perspective lenders.

You can pledge equity as collateral for a loan. Collateral is an asset owned by the individual or corporation, that can be pledged to secure a loan. In the event that the loan is not paid, the lender has the right to seize and sell the asset used as collateral. Any asset in which you or your corporation has equity can be used as collateral. This list includes real estate, stock, bonds (this can be regulated by law), business equipment, etc. You can even pledge vending machines that you have already paid for as collateral. Offering collateral often makes financing easier to find (especially in the case of poor credit) and can sometimes even result in lower interest rates. If you or your corporation does not own the asset fully you may have to obtain permission from the other partial owners. You will need to speak to a lending expert for more information on this.

Your income is the money that you gain over a period of time. Lenders, generally look at your monthly income. You need to know this number. When figuring out this number, include any paychecks, stock dividends or interest, pension income, bond payments and any annuity payments. All of these forms of income added up form your monthly income figure. Forgetting one of these categories can unnecessarily lower your monthly income figure and decrease your chances for financing.

Income Category	Dollar Value
Monthly Paychecks	$4000.00
Dividends and Interest	$750.00
Pension Checks	$0.00
Bond Payment	$500.00
Annuity Payments	$0.00
Total Income	**$5250.00 per month**

Figure 2.1 Example monthly income worksheet

Your monthly expenses are any bills that you pay monthly. Add up any rent or mortgage expenses, car payments, insurance expenses, taxes (such as property taxes), child expenses, tuition or utilities. The sum of all these bills is your total monthly expense.

Expense Category	Dollar Value
Rent/Mortgage	$1500.00
Car Payments	$300.00
Insurance	$250.00
Taxes	$300.00
Child Expenses	$0.00
Tuition	$0.00
Utilities	$250.00
Total Expenses	**$2600.00 per month**

Figure 2.2 Example monthly income worksheet

Subtracting your total monthly expenses from your total monthly income will give you your monthly disposable income. Using the numbers from Figure 2.1 and Figure 2.2:

Total Income – Total Expenses = Disposable Income

($5250.00) -   ($2600.00)   =   ($2650)

Figure 2.3 Sample disposable income calculation

This person has a disposable income of $2650 per month. This money can be used to directly invest in a vending machine enterprise. This income can also be used to guarantee monthly payments on a loan in the event of poor business performance.

These numbers will give you, not only a good idea of how much you can afford to invest, but also what kinds of loans you may qualify for.

Where to Get Start Up Money

Once you have examined your financial situation and have a good idea of your income, expenses and credit rating, you can begin to think about financing your business. If your available disposable income is large enough, you may decide to finance your vending business without borrowing by using your savings. However, even if your savings and disposable income are large enough, you may decide to borrow to finance your business. In the event that you decide to borrow, you will have a good idea of what types of loans will suit you and which you can qualify for based on your financial snapshot.

Personal Savings and Wealth

The simplest and safest way to get start up money for your new vending machine enterprise is to use your personal savings. This can be money in your savings accounts or retirement funds that can be accessed.

Before starting your enterprise, it is best to consult a qualified tax attorney or financial planner to find the best way to tap into your personal money. Missteps in this area can cost you big money in taxes and penalties, and professional advice can minimize if not eliminate these problems.

The advantages of using money that you own entirely are considerable. You generate no debt by using your money. There are no interest payments to worry about and no application process. You can access the money whenever you want and use it however you want. In short, you are in total control. Also in the unfortunate event that you must cease operating, you are not left with a debt that still needs to be paid.

Financing Sources For Your Vending Business

The subject of small business financing is a broad subject that would easily fill many volumes. The following words are designed to give you a very general idea of where to look for financing. It will be up to you to do your research and preparation carefully, but first a word of caution.

Many new businesses are unsuccessful and careless financing can contribute to these failures. All financing options need to be considered carefully and understood thoroughly. Shop around for rates and loan structures. Consult professionals and make realistic projections of sales and expenses. In short, be careful and make educated decisions.

Types of Loans

There are two main types of loans that are relevant to this book. They are the revolving credit line and the term loan.

A credit card is a type of revolving credit account. All types of revolving accounts have a fixed maximum amount that can be borrowed. If you don't use the account you don't have to pay anything except for a possible annual fee. If you do use the account you must begin to make payments of at least a minimum amount and interest charges begin to accrue. This amount is determined by the amount of the credit used and applicable lending regulations. As you pay down the amount you owe, the amount you can borrow returns to the original credit limit. An example will help.

You have qualified for a revolving credit account at a local financial institution. Your credit limit is $10000. You purchase some machines for $3000 using this credit line. Your credit limit is now $7000 and you owe $3000. Interest starts to build up as soon as you borrow the money. Lenders often offer an interest free grace period. For the purposes of this example there is no grace period. You make the minimum payment of $200 the next month. Of the $200, $15 is interest. So you have paid back $185 of the loan. This means that your credit limit is now $7185 and you still owe $2815. The next month you pay off the balance of the loan. You now owe no money and your credit limit is again $10000.

Revolving credit accounts are particularly useful to a business owner as a reserve fund. They allow you to borrow and pay interest only when you need to. In addition, they allow you to keep all of your cash invested in your business. By this I mean you do not have to keep $10000 sitting in the bank earning a small interest rate. You can invest this money in more machines and locations and borrow with your line of credit for any unforeseen expenses or sudden opportunities.

Term credit accounts are the accounts that people most often associate with borrowing. These are the accounts that are used for mortgages, car loans, and appliance purchases. A term car loan simply means that you borrow a certain amount of money and agree to pay that money back at certain set amounts (monthly payments) over a certain period called the term. Another example will make things clear.

You need to borrow $10000 to buy a van for your business. You borrow the money and agree to pay the money over a five year term. The interest rate is fixed at 6%. Your monthly payments will be 193.33. Of this amount a certain part is interest and a certain amount goes to repay the money you borrowed. At the end of the term you will have paid the amount you borrowed and will have paid interest on top of that amount as well.

Money from Family and Friends

Borrowing money from family and friends can be an awkward proposition. It can cause strains on relationships and should be handled cautiously. It is strongly advised to that you or your attorney draw up a proper promissory note that spells out the exact details of your agreement before any lending takes place. Promissory notes can be found on the Internet or you can hire an attorney to draft one. Make sure that both the lending and borrowing party sign the document and that you have the document notarized by a Notary Public. Notary Publics can be found at most copy shops and mail solutions stores. Their fees are generally quite reasonable. Both the lending and the borrowing party should receive a signed original copy and keep it somewhere safe.

The disadvantages of borrowing from friends, was mentioned earlier. It can strain relationships and turn friends into enemies. However, there are advantages as well that are similar to the advantages of using your own money. Money can be easily had because of the close relationship between borrower and lender. Interest may or may not be present and payment schedules can be more flexible. This simplicity can be of enormous benefit when getting started and is second in ease only to using your personal assets.

Commercial Banks

When someone thinks of the word "bank", they are usually thinking of a commercial bank. Commercial banks take in deposits from businesses and individuals alike and loan out those deposits. These banks deal in all kinds of loans from auto, to mortgage, to high rise construction loans. Essentially, they deal with everyone and have capital reserves large enough to make just about any kind of loan. Through economies of scale they can keep costs down on loan processing and pass that on in the form of competitive rates.

Because of their financial power and resources, commercial banks can afford to be discriminating. They are often unwilling to overlook small credit blemishes and take chances on an individual-especially one with a brand new business. At times these problems can be overcome by pledges of personal equity as collateral to loans.

Commercial banks, while cautious about loaning money to new businesses, are an excellent place to open an account for business purposes. They offer convenient access to funds through their many offices and automatic teller machines. In addition, showing that you have been a responsible and trustworthy customer over time will help with your chances of a loan in the future.

Credit Unions

Credit Unions are member-owned financial institutions. By making a small deposit (usually around $5) in an account you can often join one of these groups. Membership is often restricted by profession or the geographic area in which you live. Recently, however, these restrictions have been eased by many institutions.

Credit unions offer many types of loans similar to commercial banks, but they do not offer commercial loans as frequently as commercial banks. This varies between institutions. Some offer no commercial loans to any organization but a sole proprietorship. Some will loan to any type of business organization. As with everything else you will need to do further research in your area and see what is available. However, if you qualify, this is a good place to borrow money. While not as large as the commercial banks these institutions often offer competitive rates. In addition, these institutions are often slightly more flexible where credit blemishes are concerned, but again will be reluctant to loan large sums of money to a new business without some sort of collateral.

Again in addition to loaning money, these institutions are a good place to keep excess cash. They also offer convenient access to your money. There may be restrictions as to what types of accounts you can open depending on your business structure.

Finance Companies

Commercial banks and credit unions are the least expensive means of obtaining financing after you have determined borrowing is necessary. If these institutions are unwilling to loan you money, others can be, but at a higher price. These companies tend to charge higher rates of interest and can place a higher debt load on your fledgling company. However, properly managed and researched, these companies can offer additional options for financing.

Finance companies generally finance equipment purchases by businesses exclusively. As a general rule they do not deal with individuals. In addition, they often require specific plans for the money (e.g. I need $10000 to buy 5 machines to place at these locations). These companies often charge higher interest rates than banks and credit unions do.

These companies can be found in just about any phone book or Internet directory by looking up keywords like "equipment finance" or "equipment leasing".

Credit Cards

Credit cards can be a very expensive option for financing a new business. They are, however, an option. Many professionals would recommend against this option. Again, if diligently managed, this option can finance your business when you cannot find any other options. As with all financing options, know what you are getting into and thoroughly understand all aspect of the arrangement.

Credit cards are not at all hard to come by. You can apply online, through the mail and at any commercial bank regardless of your company structure. Your credit score will be a large factor in determining if you qualify. Also a new corporation without an established history may have difficulty in being granted credit cards.

Conclusion

The preceding pages were not intended to supply you with every detail of financing your small business. This is a very complicated subject. The intention of these pages was to give you a very broad overview of where to begin looking for money to finance your business. To help in your planning, it would be a good idea to:

✓   Get an idea of how much you are comfortable investing in a vending enterprise.
✓   Find a book on small business finance that appeals to you. As always, you can start at your local library.

- ✓ Get you credit report and credit score. Only by knowing where you stand, can you begin to plan you financing.
- ✓ Determine your net worth, disposable income, savings and equity. These numbers will be very helpful in you quest for finance.

3

Business Structures

Once you have examined your financial situation and have accurate expectations of your chances of finding financing and where you will seek it, you are ready to begin planning your business. In this section you will find information on selecting the type of business structure for your company. The various strengths and weaknesses of these structures will be discussed. In addition an explanation of the process of forming a company with each of the various structures will be provided.

The structure of your business is one of the most important decisions that you need to make during the preparation phase. The decisions you make at this point have large impacts on taxes, risk management, and estate planning as well as liability.

These are decisions that will most likely require professional advice regarding your state regulations and your personal situation. Now, hopefully, where business expenses are concerned you are careful with your financial resources. Professional advice is one of the areas that you need to be willing and prepared to spend money. The outcome of these consultations, have huge implications on your business and you want to make sure that you receive qualified guidance. Do not think of attorney's fees as expenses, but as investments in the financial health and security of your new company and your personal wealth.

The following explanations are cursory descriptions that are designed to give you only the most general understanding of various business structures and risks. Many books are available that address the issues of corporate law and each particular business structure in depth. Your local library can be a wonderful, inexpensive resource to learn all that you need on business structures before you consult an attorney.

Sole Proprietorships

By far the simplest form of business that anyone can undertake is that of the sole proprietorship. What this entails is an individual doing business an individual. The individual needs to register a business name with the state's corporations division, but that is about all that is required. There is usually a simple form to fill out and a negligible fee. Many states even allow you to do this online with a credit or debit card. There may be some additional rules or regulations that vary by state, but the whole process can be done in an afternoon.

In addition to filing papers with the state, you may need to apply for an Employer Identification Number (EIN) from the IRS, open a company bank account, buy an insurance policy, etc. All of these activities will be carried out in your name. That is to say you, John Doe, will sign his name and social security number on all business documents. You will also be personally responsible for all debts and liabilities of your company.

That last element is one that deserves further explanation. A sole proprietorship exposes its operator to a significant lawsuit risk. There is no limited liability provisions like those offered by the corporate business structures. In the event that one of your machines damages a person or someone's property you will be held personally responsible and all of your property can be forfeited in order to satisfy any judgments resulting from a lawsuit. Because of this rather large risk in a business as public as vending machines, it is a business form that is not recommend.

You and your new business will be far better served and protected by one of the business types that limit personal liability. The protection offered by these structures far outweighs the added complications and costs of their formation.

Partnerships

Partnerships are very similar to sole proprietorships in that they are simple to form and require only the smallest amount of paperwork, if any. In some cases a partnership can even be formed, in the eyes of the law, without the knowledge of the partners simply by the existence of a contract between partners. An additional similarity to sole proprietorships is the fact that partners in the partnership may be personally responsible for the debts and liabilities of the partnership.

This, again like a sole proprietorship, will put at risk your personal assets in the event of mismanagement or lawsuit. If you are considering starting a vending machine business with a partner or partners an LLC is a much safer solution and is only slightly more complicated.

If you do decide to enter into a partnership to operate your vending machine business, an attorney is essential to prepare the partnership contract to make sure that all aspects are both clear and legal.

Corporations

The concept of the corporation is one of the developments that lead to the Industrial Revolution and the modern world we enjoy today. Essentially, filing a corporation creates a new legal entity. This entity is owned indirectly by individuals known as shareholders. This legal entity has the ability to carry out business just as an individual would, but with added benefits.

One of benefits is that a corporation helps to protect personal assets. That is to say, outside of personal negligence, the only money and assets that you put at risk are the money or assets that you have invested in the corporation. This is an invaluable benefit and is the main reason many businesses are formed as a corporation.

There are several other ways in which a corporation's liability protection can be pierced. A short list of these behaviors is:

- Commingling
- Undercapitalization
- Illegal activities
- Failure to comply with corporate regulations

Commingling occurs when your personal assets and your corporation's assets are inseparable and non distinct. This occurs when you and your corporation share a bank account or when you sign your personal name on corporate documents without a qualifying title. Commingling is a very serious concern and is something to discuss in detail with your attorney at the time of incorporation. Their advice can easily eliminate this risk

Undercapitalization occurs when a corporation exists without the means to carry on its business in an independent manner. This occurs when the corporation owns nothing and has no cash on hand. This is a smaller concern than commingling but again should be discussed with your filing attorney at the time of incorporation. You will need to keep your corporation adequately funded at all times.

It is not in the interests of the state to protect your personal assets from lawsuit in conjunction with illegal activities. Corporations that engage in illegal activities put the personal assets of their shareholders at risk. This is easily defended against by making sure that your corporation complies with all laws and conducts its business in a respectable, legal manner.

The last of the mistakes one can make that will invalidate their corporate liability protection is a failure to comply with regulations. All this means, is that your state has rules governing corporations and you need to adhere to them religiously. In most states this simply means writing an operating agreement, choosing a name, and filing articles of incorporation. Annual filings will also need to be prepared. Again you will need to consult a local professional regarding the rules of you state before proceeding. In exchange for a small fee, many law firms will act as the registered agent of your corporation. They will prepare and file all of the required documents for you. The fee for this is usually reasonable and will eliminate the concern of maintaining your documents altogether.

Survivorship

Another of the benefits of a corporate business structure is survivorship. When you create a corporation you create a distinct and separate legal entity from yourself. In the event of the death of a shareholder, *such as you*, the stock in a corporation reverts to the shareholder's heir. The corporate entity is not affected by the death of one of its shareholders. This means that your business can be around long after your passing and can be a convenient tool used for estate planning.

Pass Through Taxation

Before discussing some of the various corporate types, pass through taxation needs to be explained. Pass through taxation means that the profits and losses of the corporation pass through the corporation, tax free, to the shareholders. Once the shareholders have received the profits and losses they are included in the personal tax returns of the individual. Under this system, profits are only taxed once. This system is impossible with a "C Corporation". Pass through taxation is only allowed with "S Corporations" and "LLCs".

UBI Number

If you form your company as a corporation the secretary of state where you reside, will provide your company with a unique number known as a UBI Number. UBI stands for Universal Business Identification Number. This number will uniquely identify your business and will be required in many business dealings such as opening a bank account. This number is a publicly available number and is not to be confused with the more useful, and necessary of protection, Employer Identification Number.

If you choose to operate as a sole proprietorship, you will not receive a UBI. Instead you will use your Social Security number as a means to identify your business.

Types of Corporations

The following sections list very brief descriptions of several types of corporate structures along with relevant strengths and weaknesses. This information is intended only to point you in the right direction when doing further research into the area of corporations. These pages will also allow you to ask the right questions when meeting with your attorney.

C Corporations

C Corporations are what most people thinks of when they think of corporations. Many publicly traded corporations exits as C Corporations. A C Corporation allows the type of asset protection that any corporation does. There is no limitation on the number of investors that a C Corporation can have.

There is one significant downside to C Corporation that makes it particularly unsuitable to the small business owner. A C Corporation does not allow pass through taxation. As such a C Corporation will have to file a separate tax return and pay taxes on its profits. Once its profits have been taxed those profits can be distributed to its shareholders and can be subject to additional taxation. All of these overhead and possible additional taxes are often more than a small business owner can afford to deal with. For a vending business, it makes far more sense to form as an S Corporation or as an LLC.

S Corporations

S corporations were an improvement over C corporations with the small business owner in mind. The most attractive feature of S corporations is that they do allow pass through taxation while providing the asset protection of any corporation. S corporations do have one downside. There are often limits on the amount of shareholders permitted under an S corporation. When starting a vending business, you will often find that you are the only, or one of few shareholders. This is fine at first and is even fine forty years into your business as you are retiring. However, there is no logical reason to limit the amount of investment that your business can receive by limiting the number of shareholders you can have. The next corporate type solves all of these problems and is the form that is recommended by many professionals for a small business these days.

Limited Liability Corporations (LLC)

Limited Liability Corporations offer the best of both worlds and offers the best business structure for a vending company. Limited Liability Corporations have no limits on the number of potential shareholders and offer the same liability limitation as offered by S corporations and C corporations as well as pass through taxation.

One thing to note is that the Limited Liability Corporation structure is a fairly new business structure. Most states did not have this structure until after 1990. That being said professional (attorneys and accountants) awareness of this structure is still growing. This is a great reason to do your homework. Get familiar with the requirements and advantages in your state before you contract a professional to do your paperwork. This will save you time and money and will greatly help in discussing your needs and goals with your counsel.

Forming a Corporation

Once you have selected the corporate structure that you believe is appropriate, it is time to talk to an attorney. Many paralegals and accountants will also be willing to file corporate papers for your new company. Many computer programs also exist to help with this process and you can even write your own operating agreement. However, in a matter as serious as personal wealth protection, the premier advice of an attorney is recommended.

To find an attorney you can ask friends and family for referrals, use the yellow pages, or you can take advantage of your state's bar association. The bar association is the professional association for attorney's in your state. Along with maintaining professional standards these groups also provide referral services as well as information about specific attorneys in your area. The bar association is a great place to begin your search for legal counsel.

The first and most important document that is required to form a corporation is called an Operating Agreement. This document spells out in black and white all the particulars of the corporation. These details include but are not limited to formation, accounting, rights and duties of shareholders, management, profit distribution, taxes, and dissolving the corporation. Also listed in this document are the forming shareholders, the management, main offices, effective date and a registered agent.

The registered agent is a shareholder or hired individual or company that will be responsible for receiving and answering all official communications for the corporation and preparing and filling all documents as required by the state. You can undertake this role yourself, however, in many cases for a small annual fee the law firm that does your filing will also act as your agent. The fee is very reasonable and the firm will automatically keep your annual reports and other filings up to date.

Once you have consulted with your attorney and have decided on a corporate type and your attorney has all the necessary information, you are done for a while. Your attorney will prepare your documents and send them to you for your signature. Once you have signed them you will send them to your attorney who will forward them to the secretary of state. Your attorney will most likely also submit the corporate filing fee (this can range from $50 to $500) and bill you for it later.

If everything is in order with your documents you will ultimately receive a certificate of formation listing the official name of your company along with the effective date and the UBI number. Once you have this you are the manager and shareholder of a corporation.

Employer Identification Number

An Employer Identification Number (EIN) is very similar to a Social Security Number. However, the numbered individual is generally a corporation, partnership or sole proprietorship. Your company's EIN will be used on all official documents such as tax filings, bank accounts, insurance policies and credit applications. This number will be necessary before you can attend to any of the mentioned tasks.

You will need to have formed your corporation or filed your sole proprietorship/partnership documents before requesting an EIN.

To request an EIN you can either apply online, or fill out and mail an IRS Form SS-4. The form can be downloaded from www.irs.gov or you can request one from your local IRS Office. There is no fee. If your application is approved you will be mailed your EIN in several weeks. You will need to protect this number just as you would a Social Security Number from identity thieves.

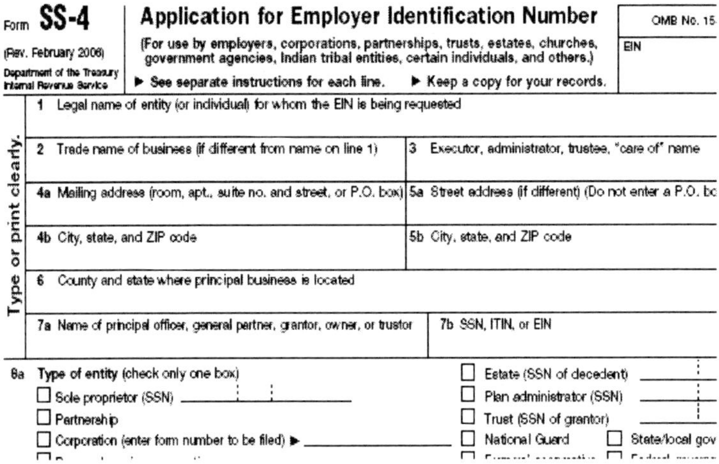
Form **SS-4**
(Rev. February 2006)
Department of the Treasury
Internal Revenue Service

Application for Employer Identification Number
(For use by employers, corporations, partnerships, trusts, estates, churches, government agencies, Indian tribal entities, certain individuals, and others.)
▶ See separate instructions for each line. ▶ Keep a copy for your records.

OMB No. 15
EIN

Type or print clearly.
1 Legal name of entity (or individual) for whom the EIN is being requested
2 Trade name of business (if different from name on line 1)
3 Executor, administrator, trustee, "care of" name
4a Mailing address (room, apt., suite no. and street, or P.O. box)
5a Street address (if different) (Do not enter a P.O. bo
4b City, state, and ZIP code
5b City, state, and ZIP code
6 County and state where principal business is located
7a Name of principal officer, general partner, grantor, owner, or trustor
7b SSN, ITIN, or EIN
8a Type of entity (check only one box)
☐ Sole proprietor (SSN)
☐ Partnership
☐ Corporation (enter form number to be filed) ▶
☐ Estate (SSN of decedent)
☐ Plan administrator (SSN)
☐ Trust (SSN of grantor)
☐ National Guard
☐ State/local gov

Figure 3.1 A Form SS-4 from the IRS will allow you to quickly and easily apply for an Employer Identification Number.

Conclusion

Now that you have a basic understanding of the various business types, you are ready to carry out more business planning. You should take a few moments and carry out the following tasks. This information will also be added to your formal business plan.

✓ Decide which type of business structure is best for your needs. Don't hesitate to talk to professionals about this.

✓ If you decide on a corporation or partnership, find a qualified attorney who is willing to prepare your documents.

✓ Come up with a list of possible business names.

✓ Download or request via mail a Form SS-4 from the IRS website or office.

4

Business Preliminaries and Risk Management

Once you have established your business, you will need to deal with some red tape before you can begin doing business. These are not especially difficult chores but will need to be done correctly to prevent headaches in the future, and risk to your personal assets and your young company.

Business Licenses

The first thing you need to attend to once you have formed your company is a business license. This basically gives your company permission to conduct business within a particular area. The best place to begin researching business licenses will be with your state's business division. The US Small Business Association (www.sba.org) is also a wealth of information regarding licenses.

You may be required to obtain a license at the state, county and city level. You may only be required to obtain a license if your gross sales are above a certain point.

Fees for business licenses are reasonable and can be tax deductible. You will most likely need to renew your license annually. You can apply for your initial license and renew online in many cases using your credit or debit card.

Once you have received you license, frame it and place it prominently wherever you conduct your business.

Professional Organizations and Publications

It is not a requirement, but finding and joining a professional organization can be very rewarding. The vending industry, like any other industry has many such organizations. These groups can be of great use to someone new to the business. These organizations offer lobbying services, networking opportunities, advice on legal affairs, consultation, industry statistics, industry news and access to trade shows.

Membership in these groups is generally open and is fairly inexpensive and well worth the cost of joining. Remember this can be a tax deductible expense in many cases. These groups can be found by doing an online search for "vending industry association". You will receive many results. Look through these and decide if any of them will suit your needs.

A great place to start is the National Automatic Merchandising Association. This is the largest vending industry association in America. Their website may be found at http://www.vending.org. This site offers many useful resources and you can join the group online.

In addition to national organizations, there are often local and regional groups as well. These can be found in a similar manner as described before. Simply add information about your state or city to the search string such as, "Iowa Vending Industry Association". Consider joining these groups as well, if they exist. These groups will be intimately acquainted with developments and needs in your particular area. This familiarity can be a wonderful asset.

In addition to professional organizations there are also a number of trade publications that may be of use to you in your new enterprise. These can be very helpful in keeping you up to date on legislation concerning the vending industry, technological developments, new products and companies, and anything else fit to print about the vending industry. You can find these online by searching for "Vending Machine Magazine". It is strongly recommended that you take advantage of these news services to keep informed about your new industry.

Permits

There are several types of permits that you may need to start your vending machine operation. Most of these permits will be for a certain period of a year to five years. You will need to keep track to your compliance with these regulations and renew when needed.

First, you will need to check with state, county and city officials to see if you need a permit to operate vending machines within their jurisdiction. It is rare but not impossible to need a city permit for each and every machine that you wish to operate in a municipal area. Each permit will cost you a fee. These fees can be considered tax deductible and are not prohibitively expensive. If theses are required make sure your company is in compliance at all times. Failure to do so can be much more expensive than the permits would have been.

If you decide to operate fresh food machines you will need a permit from either the county or city health department. Regulations concerning these permits vary wildly so you will need to check before you begin operations. You may need to obtain a permit for each fresh food machine you operate or you may only be required to buy one for your whole business. Your local health department may also have regulations pertaining to vending machines that are not fresh food machines. A simple phone call will be enough to find out. Knowing ahead of time will again prevent problems down the road.

Over the counter drug sales through your machines will also frequently require a permit. Again the local health department is your best source of information concerning local requirements. Again, you may be required to get a permit for each machine or for your company as a whole.

If your company is going to be involved in the sale of tobacco products through your machines, you will need to obtain a permit from your state's department of revenue. The state's main interest in your activities will be your compliance with state tobacco taxes. You will be required to fill out a small amount of paperwork and may be, again, required to pay a fee. If you are going to sell tobacco, you should also check with the health department again to make sure that there are no permits in addition to the permit from the department of revenue.

Opening Company Bank Accounts

Your business will be very limited in terms of what it can do until you have opened a company bank account. Most commercial banks will open business checking accounts for any type of business. Some credit unions will only open accounts for sole proprietorships. You will need to call before going into the bank or you can ask one of the customer service representatives. They will be happy to answer any questions you have.

Before walking into the bank, however, you should get all of the necessary <u>original</u> documents together in a file. A little organization will make things much easier. In most cases you will need the following documents:

- Certificate of Formation or
- Assumed Business Name Filing
- Operating Agreement
- UBI Number (This is on your certificate of formation.)
- EIN Number (This will be provided from the IRS in a letter.)

The first account that you should open is a simple business checking account. Look for one without a minimum balance or monthly fee. This will help your business keep costs low. You will need to provide some sort of initial deposit in addition to the documents listed above. If you are operating as a corporation, ask your attorney as to how you should provide this initial deposit. This will prevent any problems with commingling.

In addition to opening the account you will need to order checks as well. These will be very useful as receipts and will be helpful in tracking expenses. You should only purchase the least expensive checks that are offered, but you should get checks with carbon copies. There is no need to waste corporate money on designer checks. This money can be better invested in your young company's operations. You checks should have you company name, address, and perhaps phone numbers on them. Unless you are operating as a sole proprietorship or your name is part of your corporate identity, your personal name should not appear on your checks.

Once you have opened your checking account, you will be able to open corporate brokerage accounts and accounts with other financial companies. These will help you manage any excess cash. You will also be able to begin equipment purchases for your company and use the check copies as receipts. Later, these will be used for equipment depreciation when tax time rolls around.

Sales Taxes

With very few exceptions, if you engage in commerce in the United States, you will be required to remit sales tax revenue to state and municipal governments.

The regulations governing sales vary by state and you will need to do homework concerning your particular situation. To find out what is required, contact your local sales tax bureau. If you are unsure of where to find this agency, start with your state's department of revenue. In most cases, the agency that is responsible for collecting sales tax revenue in your area will happily mail you a comprehensive packet containing all the forms necessary to begin collecting and remitting sales tax. These forms along with helpful brochures may also be available online as well.

Risk Management

One of the primary concerns of any new business owner is risk management. The need to protect both your personal property and your new company is high in this litigious society. Many a lawyer lurks out there waiting to file a juicy lawsuit after a vending machine is tipped over on a customer, or someone gets sick, or a machine catches fire and burns down a laundry room. Now, these risks are extremely small but few business owners will remain fiscally strong should one of the events happen. Defending your company in the event of a lawsuit can tax your financial resources. Steps can be taken to protect your business and manage these risks. These should be considered.

Common Sense

Common sense is the best and cheapest protection against litigation and other business disasters. By conducting the affairs of your company in a respectable and responsible manner, you can eliminate a good portion of the potential risk to your company. Always make sure that machines are properly secured and stable. Make sure that all of your machines have stickers advising that the machines can tip and cause injury. Repair all malfunctions immediately and pay attention to expiration dates. People will do silly things in the real world and to what extent you can protect yourself simply by using your common sense will go a long way to protecting your business.

Figure 4.1 While pictures like this offer no legal protection. Informing people that the machine will not dispense free product can offer a measure of protection, not in court, but from people's stupidity.

Insurance

Insurance is the next step that you can take to protect yourself and your business. Two types of insurance will be of interest to you as a vendor. The first is general liability insurance and the other is vehicle insurance. These types of insurance policies can be very useful. Even if you are the most careful person in the world, accidents do happen and people do sue without cause. Even successfully defending your business can be a very expensive ordeal, it can be very useful to have an insurance company with its cadre of lawyers in your corner if that time comes.

General liability insurance is a type of insurance that protects against claims arising from your premises (your warehouse or office) and your product. This means that if someone slips in your warehouse or gets food poisoning from one of your sodas, this policy will help with the fallout. General liability insurance can also be augmented with many other types of coverage as well. For full details and additional coverage that can be added, you will need to speak to your insurance agent.

Vehicle coverage is pretty straightforward and is something that most people are already familiar with. This type of coverage protects against any liability resulting from a vehicle accident. You can also purchase policies that protect against vehicle theft and damage and will replace your vehicle in the event of theft or damage in an accident.

Finding an Insurance Agent

Finding a qualified insurance agent that is a good fit for you and your company can be more difficult than finding an attorney. A good place to start is your state's insurance division. This is usually part of your state's commerce department.

When actually shopping for insurance, you will need to shop around. Do not get quotes from less than five different agents. Always get quotes and offered policies in writing. Do your homework about the companies that will be issuing the policies. Have they been around for a while? Do they have a good reputation? Do the have a sound financial foundation? Do not be afraid to ask your insurance agent for customer references. Make sure that your prospective insurance agent listens to you and understands your needs. If you are not confident that they wish to sell you the policy you need rather than the policy they want to sell, find another agent.

You will want to have confidence in your agent and the company that issued the policy. When you need your insurance is not the time to find out that your insurance company has a poor reputation.

Business Policy Decisions

At this point you also need to make some decisions about your business policy. These decisions will be impact how you structure your ads, letters and phone solicitations in the following chapter.

Contracts

Deciding whether or not you are going to require contracts can be an important decision. You will need to consider this carefully. If you do decide to make use of contracts, have your attorney draw up a suitable document. You will need to decide how long the term of the contract will be and what provisions will be in it, before walking in to your lawyer's office. Usually contracts in the vending industry are for a year or less but can go a long as ten years in high volume locations.

The costs of placing a vending machine at a location can add up quickly. If you are suddenly asked to leave a location, prior to recouping your costs, you business may suffer financially. Contracts prevent this problem from occurring. Additionally, a contract can also prevent the loss of a location through competition. This can also be a benefit.

There are also arguments against contracts as well. Some business owners might ask themselves, "Why if your service is professional, do you feel the need for a contract?". Some may not like the idea of being locked in to a particular vendor. Others may not have the authority to sign a contract.

You will need to balance all these concerns and decide which is best for your business model.

Commissions

Commissions are a share of the profits that you give to the location of your vending machines. This is not an uncommon practice in the vending industry by any means and is a subject with which you should be familiar. Commissions can also be a very effective tool in securing new locations. If a business owner is on the fence about letting you place some machines, the promise of a small financial gain can often push them over the edge.

You do need to exercise some caution when offering commissions, however. It is not uncommon for new vendors to offer very high commissions automatically. Before deciding on the commission rate that your company will offer, call around to some of your competitors and try to discover what they offer. You can also find information in online resources and trade publications. This information can be invaluable. You want to use commissions as a means to secure and keep locations, but you don't want to give away the store either.

Additionally, it is not wise to offer commissions automatically. If you need to offer one to secure a location or the business owner is asking for one, that is fine. However, if the location is already secured and no one has mentioned a commission, don't bring it up. This is just an added cost that will reduce your profit margin, and should be avoided if possible.

If you decide to offer commissions make sure that you are offering a net commission. This is percentage of the money earned after all expenses have been recouped. Essentially, you are offering a share of the **PROFITS** only and not a percentage of whatever money is in the machines. Make it clear when you set up the account, how and when the money will be paid. Usually, it is best to pay the money on a monthly basis or when you service the machine. You can simply offer a check or you can count and divide the money when you are servicing the machine (Make sure you have an accurate count written down for your records). A check seems more professional, and counting money is something best done in private, but some people will insist on cash.

Conclusion

Once you have made all the decisions outlined in this chapter and have investigated all the permitting, licensing and risk management subjects also discussed in this chapter, you can begin to consider actually buying and placing machines on location. These subjects will be discussed in subsequent chapters.
At this point you should:

✓ Contact your state department of revenue and obtain information on sales tax requirements in your area.
✓ Contact your city representatives and find out what types of business licensing is required in your city.
✓ Contact you local health department and see if any permitting is required to operate vending machines within their jurisdiction.
✓ Contact several insurance agents and see what type of policies they would suggest for you and your company and how much they might cost.
✓ Contact several banks and see what they require to open a company bank account.
✓ Find two vending industry professional organizations. The Internet is the best place to do this.
✓ Decide whether or not your company is going to require contracts. If so, have an attorney draw one up.
✓ Decide if your company will offer commissions.

5

Types of Vending Operations

There are many types of vending machines that can be used by you in your business. These will be explained in this chapter along with the basics of operating these machines on your route. However a few basics details need to be covered first.

A vending machine is an automated machine that sells some type of product. That is to say it is a machine that carries on some retail business. Once we have established that, we can also determine what is not a vending machine. Any type of automated machine that does not sell a product cannot be considered a vending machine. Examples of this class of machines include coin operated laundry machines, grabbing machines, juke boxes, pay phones, internet kiosks and arcade style video games.

While healthy profits can be had from businesses involving these machines, they frequently operate on business models very different from retail vending machines. Service contracts in the coin operated laundry business can last as long as 10 years. Juke boxes and video games need software and media updates. Also, machines that employ copyrighted material such as music have licensing issues well beyond the scope of this book.

The first thing that needs to be made clear is that there are two general types of vending machines. These types are mechanical and electronic. The distinction lies in the means in which the coins are accepted. They are accepted by a device known as the coin mechanism (coin mech). This is a device that uses some sort of validation strategy to verify that the right amount of money has been deposited, and that it is valid money. A mechanical coin mech is one that uses a mechanical test. An electronic coin mech is one that uses an electronic test. Dollar bills, on the other hand, are only accepted in electronic machines, and then only by a device known as a bill validator which is separate from the coin mechanism. This is a machine that uses an electronic test to verify that the currency is valid and enough to cover the price of the desired item. A bill validator generally communicates with the computer in the vending machine in conjunction with the coin mechanism.

Mechanical vending machines often use no electricity. Usually the coin mechanism uses a type of size measurement to determine the validity o the coin. These types of machines can be fooled by slugs and do not accept dollar bills. Because of this, mechanical machines are often paired with change machines. In addition, these machines lack the ability to make any kind of change for the customer and can accept money when there is no product to sell ,although, there are often mechanical devices that prevent this.

An electronic vending machine is one that uses electricity. Through a small computer the machine has the ability to test coins (usually through capacitance or through sound), process dollar bills (with the aid of a bill validator), make change, monitor inventory, and refuse to accept money when the machine is empty. These are the classic vending machines that people think of.

<u>Figure 5.1</u> **In the left portion of the above figure a bill validator is shown from the outside of a snack machine. At right the internal unit is shown.**

Both of these types of mechanisms have been around for a long time and will continue to do so. This is because both of these types of machines have their own particular advantages. Mechanical machines can be placed anywhere. In addition to the simplicity of design, many of the mechanical models also posses a rugged reliability. Electronic machines require an outlet to plug into. This is often a concern to a cost conscious location manager. Also you have to consider things such as water damage and software updates with electronic models. Lastly, electronic machines are far more expensive than simpler mechanical machines to purchase. These machines, however, offer a great many advantages over mechanical machines. These machines make change, accept dollar bills, can sell products at different prices, and can sell a much wider array of products. These machines also look much more professional. For full size vending machines, it is strongly recommended to use only electronic machines, although mechanical models are available.

Bulk Vending

The type of vending that most people encounter first in their lives is the bulk vending machine. These were also the first types of vending machines invented.

Bulk vending is defined as the selling of any candy or food product that does not come in a package. Peanuts or gumballs are typical example of bulk vending. Bulk vending is the vending business with the highest profit **percentage**. The cost of the items sold during a bulk vending operation almost never exceed 2 cents. The minimum sale price is often 25 cents and sometimes more. By figuring a maximum cost and a minimum sale price that leaves a profit of 23 cents with and investment of 2 cents. That is over 1100% return on your capital invested!

Figure 5.2 A typical example of bulk vending machines. This machine sells candy and novelties for added profit potential.

Additionally, bulk vending is a very inexpensive way to get started. Even brand new these machines cost under $300 and in the used market good, clean machines can be had for $50 - $150. These machines have low maintenance requirements and can often be left unattended for much longer periods of time than full size vending machines. This makes them ideal for a second income source for someone who is already working in a career and has only a few hours periodically to service machines.

Lastly, these machines can even be exempt from sales tax in some states under certain circumstances.

The downside of bulk vending machines is that they have lower sales volumes than full size vending machines. While the profit margin is extremely high, the actual revenue is still a small amount. While you can make 23 cents per vend in a bulk vending machine sale a full line machine can profit 50 cents per vend. Additionally, more people use full line machines regularly than bulk vending machines. Many people use a soda or snack machine everyday but rarely purchase any bulk candy.

Hopefully, the preceding paragraph hasn't discouraged you from considering bulk vending. It is a low cost, highly profitable enterprise that would be perfect as a second income stream that you are not relying on to live. It would make an ideal means to pay for that vacation every year or save for retirement without having to rely on your salary. Bulk vending is also a great way to get a feel for the vending industry without committing your life savings.

<u>Bulk Vending Sponsorship</u>

Sponsorship is an important tool used in the bulk vending business to help in the locating of machines. Here is how it works. There are non profit organizations out there like the Vanished Children's Alliance (http://www.vca.org) that use their time and energy to help locate abducted and missing children.

These organizations use bulk vending machines to help them in two ways. Firstly, the organizations offer sponsorship stickers to vending business owners. These usually cost about $2.50 per machine per month. This money is used to fund the noble activities of these organizations. Secondly, pictures of missing children are included on the sticker. This helps to get the images of the missing children exposed to the public. When considering starting a bulk vending route, this type of partnership can be of enormous help with finding locations and it helps these fine organizations continue their work.

You will need to fill out a sponsorship application before you can receive stickers. You will also need to provide information about yourself and your company as well as your machines. This helps the charity to understand where their machines are and to protect their reputation. The whole process is usually very straightforward.

Desirable locations for bulk vending machines

Bulk vending machines really appeal to children. This means that any location suitable for a bulk vending machine should have children in or around it. You will not sell a lot of gumballs in an accounting firm downtown but will have trouble keeping the machine stocked at your local hair salon. In addition you will generally want a location where the children will be spending some time. Any type of waiting room is ideal.

Some location ideas for bulk vending machine:
- Apartment Complexes
- Beauty Salons
- Grocery Stores
- Youth Sports Facilities
- Family Restaurants
- Educational Facilities
- Recreational Centers
- Movie Theaters
- Doctor/Dentist Offices (The dentist might be a hard sell)
- Auto Mechanics Waiting Room
- Laundromats
- Office Parks
- Snack/Break Rooms
- Any kind of retail store i.e. toy or book stores

This is just a short list of the possibilities. Stopping and actually thinking about the community in which you live will undoubtedly leave you with a long list of possible locations.

Full Service Vending

Figure 5.4 Full size snack and soda machines are often paired together to increase sales. Together, these types of machines are the mainstay of the full service vending industry.

When most people think of vending machines they are thinking of full service vending machines. This type of vending includes:
- Soda
- Juices
- Sports Drinks
- Cookies
- Chips
- Candy Bars
- Ice Cream
- Sandwiches
- Dairy Products
- Sandwiches
- Cigarettes

These products are purchased often by many people and offer very lucrative investment opportunities. These products are frequently marked up 100%.

Soda Machines

Soda machines will form the backbone of any full service vending business. They are far and away the most sought after vending product out there and have an excellent profit potential. Many people buy a beverage from a soda machine on a daily basis. Some of these people will buy 3 or 4. In summer these machines will often need to be serviced daily just to keep them in business.

Types of Soda Machines

There are two types of soda machines, mechanical and electronic. Mechanical machines as were previously discussed are machines that rely on a simple non-electronic mechanism to accept and verify the money. Exact change is required, and the price is fully adjustable, but only in units of 25 cents. Mechanical soda machines do require electricity to power the compressor (the cooling unit of the machine), so they must be located near a power outlet. Many mechanical soda machines, from the exterior, look like a refrigerator with flashy images on the outside. Upon opening the door, one is confronted with the selections and coin mechanisms. These mechanical soda machines generally come in 5, 7, and 10 selections. They are reliable and simple to maintain. The downside of these machines is that they have a lower capacity than the electronic machines and lack a certain appearance that will be wanted by image conscious location managers. Also, these machines are not available through the lease programs discussed later. Lastly, the customer must either have exact change or you must affix a change machine to the unit or in the surrounding area. This will require an additional power outlet. Use them if they should happen to come into your possession but don't go out of your way to purchase them. Your money will be better invested in electronic soda machines.

Figure 5.4 Above, is pictured a full size electronic soda machine. This machine features 8 selections and does accept dollar bills.

Electronic vending machines are far more common than the mechanical machines. They are a little more complicated to maintain and repair but offer considerably higher product capacities and selections. Machines can have from 5 selections for smaller can Machines, and up to 45 for the latest glass front soda machines (these look like full size candy machines but have refrigeration capabilities and vend beverages). In addition, these machines have the ability to accept dollar bills with a bill validator and to make change through internal change reserves. The machines also offer the advantages of flexible multi-pricing, and offer a sleek professional appearance for your company.

Electronic machines are available through the lease programs that will be discussed next, and it would be strongly recommend that you your efforts on these machines. They alone have the capacities needed for profitable, high volume locations and they alone accept dollar bills. This last bit is by no means trivial and often significantly increases sales.

Lease vs. Buy

It is a well-concealed fact that the majority of vending machines in the field are owned by the soda bottlers. However, a large number of these machines are not operated by the bottlers. They exist as leased machines that are stocked and serviced by independent vending operators. How this works is explained in the following paragraphs.

Soda bottlers are constantly competing to expand their market share in any city. To that end they want to make sure that their full range of products is available in as many locations as possible. Because of this, they will offer you soda machines for a low monthly fee (usually around $20 a month) provided that you buy all of your product from them (this is not an inconvenience at all, as the bottlers usually have the best prices and product availability in town). An even better part is that this rental fee is generally waived if you buy a certain amount of soda each month per machine (usually around 10 cases). To make this arrangement even more attractive, the bottlers take care of any repairs to the machines and can quickly replace them in the event of a complete machine breakdown or break-in. This is advantageous to both you and the soda bottler. The soda bottler gets increased market share and access to locations that they may not have found otherwise. In addition, they are selling more soda through this arrangement. Lastly, you are allowed to use machines that you would otherwise have to pay for at a considerably reduced cost. This allows your company to grow faster and take on more locations than you could otherwise.

There are restrictions to this arrangement. As was already stated, if you do not buy enough product, you will have to pay the rental fee. This can add up quickly and should be avoided at all costs. In addition, you can only stock the soda products that are supplied by the bottler who provided the machine. This can cause a problem by limiting the types of beverages that you can offer in a particular machine. Of course you can always supply a machine from every bottler in town, but this will take up limited space in the location and require extra electricity. Neither of these are likely to be popular with the location. Lastly, you will need to supply your own locks. These will be discussed in later sections.

The way to get around these limitations is by owning your own beverage machines. However, beverage machines are expensive, and the costs also can add up quickly. This can limit a vending routes growth. The best solution is often to own several beverage machines. In the event that a location just insists on a specific set of products offered by competing bottlers in one machine (really a very rare problem) you can place your company's machine. However, planning to use leased machines for most locations is generally a good idea. This will allow you to grow quickly without being forced to purchase too many machines.

Bottler Serviced Machines

One other service that is frequently offered by bottlers is called "bottler serviced machines". This service can be of great value to you in your route. Essentially this type of operation has the bottler's service personnel filling and servicing the machine. You or your people are not required to provide anything other than the initial lead and the site survey. Once all of that has been completed, the bottler will place the machine and carry on the business of managing it. Your company will then receive a commission check each month or quarter (this depends on the bottler's business practices) for a percentage of the machine's sales. This will be decided at the time you set up your account with the bottler.

This type of service can be a great tool to your business. If you are limited in terms of time, to which machines you can directly service, you would be best to fill your route with the busiest and most profitable locations. Then new accounts, that do not fit this category, can be turned over to the bottler in a bottler service arrangement. This will allow you to maximize the profits of your directly served route and profit from accounts that you would not otherwise have time to manage.

Soda Machine Profit Potential

Now, the profit potential of beverage vending has already been hinted at. Usually the units sold in these machines at wholesale cost around $.35 or so for a 12 oz can and $.60 or so for a 20 oz plastic bottle. Common sale prices are $.50-$1.00 for 12 oz cans and $1-$1.50 for 20 oz bottles. That means that profit margins are somewhere between 85-100%. That isn't bad at all and will again beat anything Wall Street has to offer. Also, if you have a beverage machine and a snack machine next to each other in say, a laundromat, you will almost always carry out tremendously more beverage sales than candy sales. Often in summer you will have to stock these machines several times a week if not daily to keep them in business.

Locations for beverage machines

Just about anywhere people spend any time is a good location for a soda machine, but that doesn't mean just anywhere. Usually you want to make sure that there are at least 20 people in the area on a daily basis. A beauty salon that has one stylist and brings in about 6 customers a day is not a good place to put your machine. You will almost never sell enough soda to cover your lease fee, let alone enough to waive it. Use common sense when placing machines.

Children again are a great thing to have in or near a location. All of the places that were listed for bulk vending machines will work for soda machines as well but you can add these to your list (These locations will work for most full line vending machines):
- Office Parks
- Machine Shops
- Factories
- Warehouses
- Wholesale Suppliers
- Construction Sites (these can be temporary but very lucrative in summer)
- Construction Suppliers (concrete, lumberyards etc.)
- Rental Equipment Facilities
- Plant Nurseries
- Gas Stations
- Apartment Laundry Rooms

- Hotels/Motels
- Churches

As was stated earlier, beverage vending is the mainstay of the vending industry and should make up the bulk of your operations.

Snack Vending

Snack vending is the second largest class of machines in the vending industry. Snack machines almost always exist in tandem with beverage machines as a means to increase revenue and you will rarely be asked to provide only a snack machine.

What kind of snack machines are out there?
Again as with beverage machines, there are both electronic and mechanical machines. The mechanical machines generally have a coin mechanism for each item selection and a central coin box. They do not make any change and are generally best used in conjunction with a change machine. Prices are adjustable and you can set a different price for every coin mechanism. The selections on these machines are generally smaller, usually no more that 20.

Figure 5.6 The above image shows a typical "tabletop" snack machine. This machine features 10 mechanical selections. These types of machines are ideal for offices too small for a full size machine.

Electronic snack machines, as shown in Figure 5.7 below, offer many more options. They accept dollar bills, support multi-pricing, make change, and offer many more selections. The prices on these machines are customizable and can be incremented as high as $99.95 in many cases

Figure 5.7 This is a typical example of a multi-selection and multi-price snack machine. This machine features various sizes of coils to allow a variety of product to be sold.

So where can I lease one?

Snack machines, as a general rule, are not offered through the lease programs like soda machines. The difference between the candy and soda industries is that many different companies produce many different products that can be sold through snack machines. No single company exists that can supply all the product you need to stock a snack machine to the satisfaction of your customers. As a result no company has enough motivation to put together a machine lease program.

So if I can't lease one what do I do?

This does not mean that you should avoid snack machines or cannot afford them on your new route. Many very nice snack machines can be had a very reasonable prices through the used market. Good places to purchase these machines are through classified ads, online auctions, local vending machine dealers, or other vending companies. One thing to keep in mind is these machines are heavy and freight charges can be expensive. It is best to conduct your business locally and to cultivate local sources of good, used snack machines.

Snack Machine Profit Potential

These machines, even when you have to pay for them, can still be very profitable. Many of the items that you need to stock this type of machines can be purchased for $.30-$.60 and sold from $.50-$1.25. This is also a very healthy profit margin, and when coupled with a soda machine sales can go even higher.

In addition, these machines offer opportunities to sell more than just snacks and candy. It is entirely possible to sell:
- Nonprescription drugs
- Diapers
- Shampoo
- Shaving equipment
- First aid supplies
- Maps
- Sunglasses
- Cigarette Lighters
- Deodorant
- Laundry detergent
- Prepaid phone cards
- Cigarettes (This is only permissible in age controlled environments such as bars)

The possibilities are fairly unending. You can easily adjust the shelves in the machines to allow you to sell whatever product is warranted by the location's business or its customers. You can also add attachments to snack machines that allow frozen food sales, and even soda sales.

Frozen Food Machines

There are two types of vending machines that sell frozen food. The first of these machines is a stand alone machine that behaves similarly to snack machine but with a cooling system and seal to keep the cold in.

Figure 5.8 The inside compartment of a frozen food machine. Notice the gasket around the door to keep the product cold.

It is also common to see a frozen food machine connected to a snack machine. These machines look like a snack machine with a cooling system but lack keypads and money slot. They work by utilizing the computer, keypad and money systems in the host snack machine through an electronic connection. Before buying an add-on frozen food machine, you will need to make sure that you have a suitable snack machine with which to pair it.

Figure 5.8 A frozen food machine attached to a host snack machine.

Cigarette Vending

It used to be the case that cigarette machines were commonplace in the vending industry. This is no longer true. You will be hard pressed to find a specifically designed cigarette machine. With the ability of snack machines to sell such a wide variety of products, there is simply no need to make a machine solely for the purpose of selling cigarettes.

All that is needed to convert a snack machine into a cigarette machine is a little price adjustment. It would also be very helpful if your bill validator accepted bills larger than $1 as well.

As far as locations for cigarette machines, this is a little trickier. You cannot simply sell cigarettes anywhere. Cigarettes can only be sold in areas where you can be assured that your patrons are over 18. If a minor does purchase cigarettes from one of your machines, you may be held legally responsible. This will mean expensive fines and other possible penalties. This narrows the field quite a bit. Good examples of possible locations are:

- Bars
- Nightclubs
- Over 18 clubs
- Over 18 juice bars
- Adult boutiques
- Over 18 concert venues

These are about the only locations that cigarettes can safely be sold. However, the profit potential will make searching for these locations a good idea.

Another consideration when selling tobacco products is the potential need of additional licensing. It is a good idea to consult both your local county health department and your state department of revenue to see what regulations, if any, exist in your area. If you do need any form of licensing, a simple fee and some paperwork is usually all that is required.

Hot Beverage Machines

Hot beverage machines are another class of vending machines that may be of interest to you and your young company. These machines dispense hot beverages such as coffee, hot chocolate or tea. These machines can even offer hot soups in some cases.

Hot beverage machines are outwardly similar to other vending machines as far as customers are concerned. They can accept bills through a bill validator or coins through a coin mechanism. Inside, the machines are markedly different from other full size vending machines. These machines, instead of prepackaged sodas or snacks, grind fresh coffee beans or utilize dehydrated mixes and add hot water. The resulting beverage or soup is then dispensed in an open container. This container can either be supplied through the machines internal cup reserve or the cup can be provided by the customer.

The hot water is supplied through an internal hot water heater. The actual water is supplied by an attachment to an external water supply. The water is then heated using the water heater which is powered through the 110 volt outlet.

The need to attach the machine to an external water line will be an added complication in adding these machines to your route. Unless you are an experienced plumber, you should make use of a plumbing subcontractor. This will also make it difficult to prove personal negligence in the event of a plumbing problem. The cost of a plumber is also a tax deductible expense.

These machines are supplied by most of the major vending machine manufacturers in a variety of models. You can buy machines that simply offer traditional coffee options or you can purchase machines that offer all of the trendiest Italian specialty coffees with flavor options as well as dispensing hot chocolate, tea and soups. This class of machines is also offered in standard sizes as well as compact and table top models. This type of vending machine can also be found paired with a snack machine. The two machines are controlled by a central computer and bill validator.

Offices and waiting areas are the best places to locate these machines. In addition these machines are not available through lease programs. They can be found for $750 to $2000 in the used markets. This type of machine, because of the added expense of installation and purchase of the machine makes them only appropriate for larger locations but they can be a useful addition to your machine inventory.

Novelty Vending

Novelty machines are used to sell a wide variety of products. These machines are usually located in the bathrooms of a business such as a bar or nightclub. The majority of these machines are used to sell condoms but other products such as perfume and cologne, emergency deodorant, over-the-counter drugs, stickers and other novelty items are sold as well.

These machines are generally mechanical and only accept quarters. Each item is held in a separate stack from the other items and each item has a separate coin mechanism. These individual coin mechanisms can each be set to a different price depending on the item.

These machines, purchased new, can be several hundred dollars. However, again looking in the used market or online, you can find very good deals. Since these machines can be shipped due to their lower weight, you are not limited in where you can look.

These machines have excellent profit margins frequently near 80%, however, the sales volume of this category of vending tends to be lower. You will only need to service these machines biweekly or monthly. As such they offer an excellent investment opportunity for an individual who does not have a lot of spare time.

Fresh Food Vending

Fresh food vending involves selling freshly made items that can spoil. This includes sandwiches, salads and the like. This type of vending can be difficult and is not recommended for the beginner. It involves regimented product freshness management and licensed kitchens in which to prepare the food. This can be costly and cumbersome. In addition only the busiest of locations can support this type of vending. Smaller locations will not sell enough to justify the time and cost for a beginning operator. Once your company has grown to a powerhouse of the local vending community or if you wish to expand into catering you can consider this option.

Change Machines

Every effort should be made to acquire vending machines that have bill validators. These will ensure that your route is as profitable as it can be and will also offer the highest level of convenience to your customers. There are, however, perfectly good machines out there that do not have bill validators on them. These machines are older but are very reliable workhorse machines suitable for lower profile locations such as industrial facilities. These types of machines make change machines necessary. Change machines are machines that do not vend anything and create no revenue. All they do is accept paper money and convert it to coins. These coins can then be used to purchase items from the machines that do not accept bills.

There are many manufacturers for these machines out there and many options are available. In casinos it is not uncommon to see these machines accepting large denomination bills and turning them into nickels or quarters. For the vending industry, it is primarily important to have change machines that accept $1s and $5s and offer change in quarters, dimes and nickels.

There are two classes of machines that are common. These are the "full size" change machines and the "add on" change machines.

The full size change machine is a four foot tall floor model that is used in high volume locations. These machines are heavy duty and high capacity. Some machines boast a capacity of 20,000 coins! Larger machines commonly only make change into one type of coin such as quarters or dollar coins. Some of these machines will even convert large bills into smaller bills *and* coins for the convenience of your customers. As these machines cost several thousand dollars and can hold up to $20,000 in dollar coins, they are completely unsuitable for all but the most secure locations.

The "add on" change machine is a much smaller, lower capacity, and less expensive model that is secured to the side of a host machine. Generally a series of bolts is used for this purpose. These machines are generally under 24 inches in height and do not weigh more that 75 lbs. Theses smaller models can hold dimes, nickels, and quarters and almost always have a capacity under $300 dollars. The security features of these machines vary across model types. Some machines have nothing for security but a simple hasp lock. Other machines have t-handle locks that can be equipped with the same security features described for full size machines. The fact does remain that these machines are small and easily moved by an individual. Once separated from the host machine little would stop a thief from absconding with your company's property. Therefore, again these machines should only be used at locations that are considered secure. Never utilize a change machine at a location with 24 hour access. In that situation a newer machine with a built in bill validator and sophisticated security features is a better choice.

Conclusion

Now that you have a basic understanding of the types of machines that will be used on your route, you can also begin to give consideration to the types of products you wish to sell. At this point in your preparation it would be helpful for you to:

- ✓ Decide which type of machine(s) you wish to start your route with and how many of them you will need.
- ✓ Contact your local soda bottlers and get information on their lease and bottler serviced machine programs.
- ✓ Find the local vending machine distributors. The phone book will be the easiest way in most cases.
- ✓ Compare prices and estimate how much you think you will need to invest in machines to start your route.

6

Service Vehicles

In addition to your actual vending machines, a vehicle for your business will be essential. Your service vehicle will be your mobile office and can be a mobile warehouse. As such it is very important that your vehicles be efficient reliable machines. However, it is very easy to drain your company accounts outfitting such a vehicle. What follows is some advice on finding a reliable, inexpensive vehicle, and how to equip it to best suit your needs. This vehicle will be one of your most important company assets. Without it, it will be very difficult to service your machines.

Five types of vehicles are particularly useful in the vending industry. These are the step van, the pickup truck, the cargo van, the mini van and the box truck. The strengths and weaknesses of each of these vehicles are discussed in this chapter.

Step Vans

Step vans are a very common type of vehicle in commercial service fleets. They are frequently utilized by businesses that need mobile shops or service areas (like kitchens) as they can accommodate machinery and equipment and be outfitted with power systems and water supplies. Step vans offer a great deal of product space for supplying your machines and offer the advantages of having all of your repair equipment and replacement parts immediately on hand in the event they are needed.

Step vans are commonly available with either gasoline of diesel engines and this can affect their fuel economy. For a 10000 gross vehicle weight (GVW) you can expect around 10 mpg for a gasoline engine and 14 mpg for a diesel engine. A truck with 10000 GVW should be sufficient for all but the largest vending routes.

While step vans can be very useful to larger routes, they may not be the ideal vehicle for a smaller operator. The large hauling capability of a step van may not be needed on a smaller route. This means that the larger, more powerful engines are unnecessary and can dramatically increase the cost per mile of your vehicle.

The other downside of a step van for a smaller operator is that they are more expensive than smaller vehicles. A new operator would be wise to consider investing their capital in more machines than in vehicles with unused capacity.

Figure 6.1 A typical example of a step van. Step vans can be used to hold all your product as well as repair tools and spare parts.

Cargo Vans

Cargo vans are vans that are smaller than step vans but larger than minivans. They offer many of the same advantages of step vans but can offer more fuel economy. The trade off is that they offer less space to carry product. However, in reality the average cargo compartment is around 250 cubic feet and will offer plenty of space for small to medium routes.

Modern cargo vans are also available with gasoline or diesel engines. Both of these types of engines commonly offer around 15-20 mpg. This is a distinct improvement over a step van and with future gas prices being uncertain, this can offer significant potential savings over the life of the vehicle.

Cargo vans offer the best of all worlds for a smaller operator. Their cargo capacity will be sufficient to haul all of the product to keep your machines supplied. In addition to their cargo capacity, the heavy duty engines of cargo vans, when paired with a trailer, can make a very efficient system for moving your machines as well.

Towing capacities of cargo vans range from 8000 – 10000 pounds and will easily handle several vending machines and a heavy duty trailer.

Cargo vans with shelving can be easily and inexpensively obtained. Large numbers of these vans are used by craftsmen of all types and are often sold at reasonable prices when they are several years old. If well maintained these vehicles can offer years of efficient, reliable service.

Figure 6.2 This typical example of a cargo van shows the large cargo section of this type of vehicle.

Mini Vans

Figure 6.3 Minivans offer many of the advantages of cargo vans with increased fuel economy.

Mini vans are a step down from the cargo van. These vans employ a lighter truck chassis than cargo vans and have a slightly smaller hauling capacity. Fuel economies on these vehicles are usually between 15-20 miles per gallon. These vehicles also usually come equipped with a gasoline engine. As a general rule diesel engines are hard to come by, if not impossible. Again like cargo vans, these vehicles are frequently used by tradesman because of their cargo compartments. These can also be outfitted with shelving.

While there is a smaller hauling capacity with these vans, they are very common and inexpensive. This combined with their cargo capacity and the ability to add shelves makes them an attractive option to the new vending entrepreneur.

Pick Up Trucks

Figure 6.4 Pickup trucks can be very useful in moving machines, but are impractical for servicing machines.

Pick up trucks are particularly useful to a vending machine operator as a means to move machines. They can be used to transport product but offer considerably less space than step vans or cargo vans. In addition, to protect your product from sun and rain you will need to use a truck canopy that can be added and removed as necessary. A canopy will not necessarily protect your product from summer heat and winter cold. This makes pick up trucks a less than ideal choice for your primary service vehicle.

It is possible to use a trailer in addition to your pickup truck to haul product. In practice, this setup would be more trouble than it is worth. A van of some type should be your primary route vehicle. A pickup truck should be added only when you are moving enough machines to justify the insurance, storage, and maintenance costs of dedicated moving vehicle. Until you reach this point you can rent trucks to move your machines as needed and avoid the additional overhead.

Pick up trucks are also commonly available in either diesel or gasoline models. The fuel economy and towing statistics of pickup trucks are similar to cargo vans.

Like the other vehicles that have been previously discussed, used pickup trucks can be easily found in most cities at reasonable prices.

Box Trucks

Figure 6.5 Box trucks are ideal for moving machines and have powerful engines, but have a low fuel economy.

Box trucks are the quintessential moving truck. They have a large hauling capacity and often have a 25000 GVW ratings. These trucks are very good for moving machines and often come preloaded with lift gates.

Figure 6.6 Lift gates make the loading and unloading of machines very simple. They are a common feature on box truck but can be added to pickups and even cargo vans.

The best use of these vehicles is again, as a means to move your machines. They can also be outfitted with ramps and shelves that would facilitate easy loading and unloading of supplies for servicing machines.

The trade off for the dramatically increased hauling capacity of these vehicles is lower miles per gallon. A truck with a 10 foot box with a gasoline engine will get around 12 mpg, while a 26 foot box truck will get between 6 – 8 mpg with either a gasoline or diesel engine.

Vehicles of this type, that fit the needs of your company are somewhat harder to find used but by no means impossible. A great place to check is with the truck rental companies themselves. Each of these companies has to maintain a well managed and professional looking rental fleet that has no place for worn cabs and aged paint. As such, they often sell vehicles that are slightly older than they can tolerate. These trucks are still in serviceable condition and can be had at very reasonable prices.

Trailers

Trailers can be a very useful addition to your fleet and are worth considering. The best use of a trailer is for moving your machines around town.

You will need to ensure that the trailer will be suitable for your purposes before you buy it. You should determine the maximum number of machines that it can haul by checking the trailer's weight capacity and thoroughly reading the trailer's owner's manual. You will also need to make sure that the towing package on your primary vehicle will be able to tow your trailer fully loaded with vending machines. Again, this information can be found in the owner's manual. One other thing that you need to be sure of is that the trailer will be able to haul your machines safely. To this end you should only buy a trailer with side rails and tie down supports. This will greatly increase the safety of your trailer.

New Vs. Used. Which is right for your company?

The question of whether to buy a new service vehicle or a used one, can be a tough question for a new business owner. When first starting out it is easy enough to convince yourself that you need the latest and greatest vehicle that money can buy. However, an important practice when just starting out is to shepherd your cash reserves and to not buy things that are not truly necessary. To that end consider the following items before buying a vehicle:

- Don't buy more vehicle than you need. Try to be as precise as possible in estimating the amount of product you will be hauling. Overestimating your needs can cost you big money through wasted fuel.
- Don't let vanity cost you big bucks. It is possible to convey a thoroughly professional image without buying the most expensive brand new service vehicle.
- If you do decide to buy a used vehicle make sure that it is reliable by having it inspected by a professional mechanic to protect your investment.

If you decide to buy a new vehicle, finding a commercial truck dealership is very easy. Simply consult your local yellow pages. If you decide to purchase a used vehicle the following is a list of good places to look:

- Newspaper classifieds
- Online ad spaces
- Truck/Car rental companies
- Municipal auctions
- Charity auctions
- Used vehicle dealerships
- Towing companies
- Mechanics
- Other vending companies

Outfitting your rig

Once you have decided on, and purchased a vehicle, you need to fill it with all the items you will need in the field. Below you will find a list of useful items to take with you:

- ✓ Screwdrivers (Phillips and flathead)
- ✓ Claw Hammer
- ✓ Allen Wrenches
- ✓ Watch Screwdrivers
- ✓ Mallet
- ✓ Wrench
- ✓ Pliers
- ✓ Socket Wrench
- ✓ Level
- ✓ Electric Drill/Screwdriver
- ✓ Tape Measure
- ✓ Box knife
- ✓ Duct tape
- ✓ WD-40
- ✓ Permanent Marker
- ✓ All Purpose Cleaner in a spray bottle
- ✓ Window cleaner
- ✓ Flash light
- ✓ Batteries for the flashlight
- ✓ Paper Towels
- ✓ Vinyl scrubber
- ✓ Tool box
- ✓ Cloth rags
- ✓ Electrical Tape
- ✓ Safe (This is optional but can be useful)
- ✓ Clipboard and clipboard rack
- ✓ Extra locks of all kinds
- ✓ Key locker
- ✓ First Aid Kit (This will be handy!)
- ✓ 3 ring binder with copies of your machine repair manuals
- ✓ Multimeter (This is used to test for electricity)
- ✓ Garbage Bags

This is merely a suggested list of items that you will find useful in your business activities, add items as necessary.

Conclusion

Now that you are familiar with the vehicle types that are useful to the vending industry, you can begin to research and plan your service fleet. To help in this you should:

- ✓ Decide which types of vehicles would be appropriate for the goals you set in Chapter 1.
- ✓ Decide on an appropriate budget for your service fleet.
- ✓ Begin to look in your local newspaper or local online advertisements for these types of vehicles.
- ✓ Save advertisements of the types of vehicles you are looking for in your price range. These may be available when you choose to buy or the dealerships that are offering them may be a good source of vehicles in the future.
- ✓ Find a mechanic that you decide is reliable and that offers pre-purchase inspections at reasonable prices.

7

Finding Locations

Finding locations is crucial to your success in the vending industry. Without locations you cannot sell any products or more importantly – make any money. In the following pages several time tested and effective ways of finding locations will be explained. The best part about these is that they are designed for a small business advertising budget and won't break your bank. Several of these are also passive techniques that can be turned on and off cheaply and easily as the needs of your business dictate.

Turn-Key Vending Businesses

What may seem the easiest option to start in the vending industry is called a "turn key route". When looking to buy vending machines, locations or routes, you will often encounter advertisements for high volume routes and locations that are prepackaged for you. The idea is that all of the work has been done for you in assembling the route and you just need to buy the business and start raking in the money. This is similar to franchising, but no relationship between the organizing company and yours exists once the sale is complete. No further support should be expected. A great deal of caution should be exercised when exploring this option. Some of the companies that are selling these "routes" are simply selling overpriced, ineffective machines on locations that are slow to worthless. Many a new vendor has lost their entire capital in these deals and been forced to leave the industry. If you have enough money to start again and reorganize, you will have learned an expensive lesson.

This is not to say that some of these opportunities are not worth exploring and seriously considering. Don't let a few bad apples spoil the bunch. Do your homework and remember the proverbs of "Buyer beware!" and "If it sounds too good to be true, it probably is.".

It's Not What You Know But Who You Know

The easiest way to find a location, without buying it, is often the one that people most commonly overlook. That is to say your friends and family offer some invaluable opportunities to find locations for your vending machines. It would be safe to say that most of your friends and relatives are employed in one way or another. That being said, it is rare they will work in a little office all alone without any people, and they already know the boss on a personal level. A simple suggestion from one of these people about the need for a soda or snack machine can often be enough to provide you with a location. If you combine this technique with the next idea you have a very effective combination.

Sign-Up Bonuses

One of the most effective methods for finding vending machine locations is the "sign-up" bonus. A sign-up bonus is a gift of some kind for having secured the location for your company. Some companies will send over a couple of cases of free soda and candy. Another inexpensive idea is buying a pizza lunch for the employees on the Friday the week the machines are delivered. However, the most effective sign-up bonus is often cold hard cash.

The beauty of the sign up bonus is that you can use it as a hook in your advertising campaigns as well. Say for example you placed a yellow pages ad. Consider the words "Ask about our sign-up bonus!", at the bottom of your ad. This can create curiosity in a potential customer who might not have called you before. This same technique can be applied to fliers, direct mail envelopes, cold calling, and any print advertising.

Fifty to one hundred dollars is generally an effective amount to get anything that isn't illegal. Most people out there will be happy to take a survey or test a product for an amount in this range. Asking their boss about getting a new soda machine will seem like a minor inconvenience if they will receive a cash "thank you" for doing it.

Direct Mail Campaigns

Direct mail campaigns often have bad connotations. Many people out there refer to them as "Junk Mail" campaigns. If direct mail campaigns did not work you would never receive any catalogs, credit card offers, surveys or coupons. The fact that you do receive them and probably have for most of your life says that there is something to them. Every year many large companies spend millions in postage and printing costs just to fill your mailbox. There is no reason that as a small business you cannot take advantage of this same winning strategy.

The first thing that you need to get started in direct mailing is a mailing list. These can be purchased for a small fee for each name on the list. If this avenue interests you type "Mailing Lists" into any online search engine. You will find many companies willing to supply you with professionally generated lists of names that fit any criteria you specify. The downside to this approach is that costs can add up quickly.

By doing a little work you can eliminate much of the cost of a direct mail campaign. The first thing that you should do is sit down and make a list of twenty location types that would be good for vending machines. Once you have finished that list, go to a free online yellow pages site. One at a time type the location category names into the site and look at all the names of businesses, addresses, and phone numbers you get for free! A sample list of location ideas follows:

Direct Mail Category List

- Apartment Complexes
- Warehouse and Office Parks
- Auto Repair
- Medical Offices
- Banks and Credit Unions
- Construction Supply/Lumber Yards
- Hotels/Motels
- Schools (By this it is meant trade schools such as "Massage School" or "Real Estate School")
- Print Shops
- Machine Shops
- Trucking Companies
- Car/Truck Rental and Sales Lots

- Fitness Centers/Gyms/Recreation Centers
- Car Washes
- Mini Storage Businesses
- Garden Centers and Nurseries
- Hair Salons
- Churches
- Laundromats
- New Business Listings
- Distributors of any kind

The last two need a little explaining but they can both be a rich source of locations.

New businesses are often listed in local "business weekly" types of newspapers. These are compiled from publicly available municipal databases. Few of these businesses will have vending machines and often can be secured with little effort. You just need to get to these new businesses first.

Distributors are companies that have large warehouses filled with product to sell. To manage all of the pallets requires lots of warehouse workers and truck drivers. All these hard working people often enjoy a soda and snack making these businesses excellent locations for vending machines.

Once you have compiled your list of potential locations, the next thing you need to do is design both an envelope and a letter to send to these businesses. You can keep it simple and just send a plain envelope and plain paper letter; it is much more effective, however, to make use of a logo and letterhead. These can often be designed and produced at very reasonable prices at local print shops. Make sure that your phone number and email address are clearly listed in the letterhead. One additional suggestion is to put some kind of phrase that alerts the recipient to the sign up bonus, if you are offering them. Place this message beneath the address space. This can often make the difference between your letter winding up in the garbage can, or being read and turning into a new location.

Your letter should be simple and direct. If you have actually convinced someone to open your letter you are not going to get much more of their time. In the first paragraph you should state that you want place a soda or snack machine at the business and the details of the sign up bonus. Once those ideas are out of the way you can explain all the other details. Under no circumstances should the letter be more than 3-4 paragraphs. Remember to keep it short and to the point.

Once you have completed all of these tasks you can actually start mailing them. There should be an overall strategy to this. If you have a list of 1000 business names don't send them all out at once. What happens in the remote chance that they all say "yes"? If you are a new business it would be very hard for you to meet all those obligations and make all of these new customers happy. Even fifty positive responses would be difficult to manage over a two week period. What you need to do is mail out a few each week and see what happens. Try sending out 10-20 a week to start and then move on from there. At current postage rates that will cost you no more than about $10 a week.

Take it slowly and see what happens. If you are doing well, and you get a 10% response each week, you will be busy adding machines to your route for some time to come.

Figure 7.1 **An example of a direct mail letter. Include your contact information at the top of the letter.**

ABC Vending
123 Any Street
Any Town USA 12345
555-555-5555

Dear Manager;

Thank you very much for taking the time to read this letter. ABC Vending would like to place a soda machine at your business. As a "Thank You" for this, ABC Vending will provide your office with a Friday pizza party.

ABC Vending is a professional vending machine company and the addition of one of our machines to your business can be of benefit to you as well. Adding our clean, professional looking machines to your location offers a valuable service to you, your employees, and your customers at no cost to you. This can increase both productivity and customer satisfaction.

Please call 555-555-5555 at your convenience to learn more. One of our route managers will quickly visit your business to get you set up.

Thank You;
Your Signature

John Doe
ABC Vending Manager

Another added bonus of a self directed direct mail campaign is that you can use this tool when and if you need it. If you have extra cash lying around and would like to add a machine to your route, simply start sending out letters. If your response has been overwhelming, stop sending out letters while you get all the new locations set up.

Cold Calling Prospective Customers

The same list that you generated for your direct mail campaign can also be used for cold calling. Cold calling is another technique that many consumers are not fond of, but still works. For those of you who are unfamiliar with the term, cold calling is an unsolicited sales call to a business. During this call you try to convince the business manager to meet with you to discuss locating a vending machine in more detail.

One of the most important things to have before you begin cold calling (in addition to your phone list) is a script. Before you call anyone sit down and write a short script that you are comfortable saying to a manager. This script, like the direct mail letter should be short and to the point. Say only what you need to say. An example script is:

Hello. My name is (Your name) and I am calling from (Your Company Name). We are currently looking to place soda and snack machines in your area. We are currently offering a pizza party sign-up bonus for all new accounts. Is that something you would be interested in?

Make sure that this script is something that you are comfortable saying. The above paragraph is just a guide that you are free to modify it to your comfort level. Be articulate. Make sure that you can say the whole script without pausing and saying "uh" incessantly. Make sure it sounds natural and unrehearsed coming out of your mouth.

To actually cold call someone, sit down and take a deep breath. Dial the number and ask for the manager. Once the manager answers, start reading the script. Ideally the entire script would be read to the business manager/owner right away. Once you have asked the question "Is that something you would be interested in?", wait for their response. They may think for a moment, but will answer you quickly.

More often than not, the manager will decline. Get used to this fact. Cold calling can be difficult and frustrating, but it does work. The easiest way to use cold calling to find locations without getting discouraged is to set goals. Make a deal with yourself that you will cold call twenty potential customers a day. You can also make a deal with yourself that you will find one lead a week through cold calling. Both of these are very easy to do. In addition a list of only 3000 business names will keep you cold calling every business day for a year and then some. The last benefit of cold calling is that, other than the cost of the phone line, cold calling is free.

Fliers and Posters

Free community bulletin boards are very common and easy to locate. Putting together a simple print ad using inexpensive printer paper and making 100 copies will cost you less than $10. Place them on any community bulletin board that you can find and at only 7-10 cents each, you have very little to lose. Some places to find community bulletin boards include:

- Grocery stores
- Churches

- Recreation centers
- Colleges
- Libraries
- Clubs
- Apartment complex clubhouses and laundromats
- Public facilities such as pools, parks, and golf courses

In addition to the inexpensive fliers, you can easily advertise on your already placed machines and service vehicles. Each full size vending machine offers many square feet of advertising space as does any van or truck. Why not use this to your advantage by turning each and every one of your customers or fellow drivers into your next business lead? Using inexpensive software you can design a large poster type ad. Using this computer file, you can have it printed with an adhesive or magnetic backing. These can be easily affixed to your equipment and removed with little trouble. The cost of the printing is low and you can reuse these advertisements as you need them.

If you are using leased machines you will need to make sure that advertising on them is permitted before you place an ad. Failure to check before placing an ad could be an unfortunate mistake.

Online advertising

Online advertising is a rapidly growing segment of the business world. That being said, there are many well known, heavily trafficked sites that will offer you free text advertising. If you are unfamiliar with these you can search for "free text ads" or "free community ads" in an online search engine. Local newspapers also frequently offer online classified ads. All you need is an email address and a computer. Since these classifieds are free you can use them as much as you want and post to as many sites as you want. See what happens and try it out. Do some experimenting and find out what works in your area. You can find these forums by typing your city name, or the name of a major city near you, and the phrase "free classifieds" into any of the major search engines.

Websites

Another type of advertising you should consider is setting up a website. The subject of internet publishing is a very broad one and is beyond the scope of this book. If you are not a computer expert you can have a professional looking website designed for under $500.

Without promotion, your site will have little chance of being stumbled on by a random Internet user. The advantages of a website are that you can list it on any business cards and letterhead that you produce to act as an online brochure. Stylish pictures and carefully worded text can do a great deal to supplement any other advertising.

To publish your website on the Internet, you will need a hosting company. A hosting company is a company that sells space on their computers which are specifically designed to distribute webpages over the Internet. If you are not sure which company to sign up with, you can either search on the Internet for "hosting company" or ask your website designer for a recommendation.

Another added bonus of a hosting company is that you often receive a free email address that is associated with the name of your website. It often looks much more professional to see *"yourname@yourwebsite"* rather than *"yourname@freeemail"*.

Business Cards

Business cards can be a very useful tool in promoting the services of your company. You can place them on bulletin boards, include them in direct mailings, and hand them out to prospective location managers.

Business cards are very easy to come by. You can find free, easy to use design software online. You can also gather business cards with designs you like and take these cards to a local print shop. From these examples they can help you design cards that fit your needs. Many of the online vendors will offer you a very inexpensive initial lot of cards to win your long term business. This is worth considering.

Business cards are usually printed in lots starting at 250. Make sure that their design is acceptable and all the information is correct before printing. Once they are printed to your specifications you are obligated to pay for them.

Print Advertising

Print advertising refers to any type of advertising that is printed. Where the vending industry is concerned this generally means advertising in either the yellow pages or in newspapers.

Print advertising can be very effective but can be more costly than previous options. This does not mean that you, as a small business owner, cannot mount a print advertising campaign. What the higher cost of print advertising does imply is that you need to pay attention to budgeting and spending limits. Before writing your ads and finding the media in which to show them to the world, sit down and decide how much you can reasonably spend and stick to it.

All newspapers have an advertising department that will be happy to discuss all of their different advertising options. There will be many different sizes of ad space that the newspaper sells. You will need to weigh the cost and size of each of these ads against the amount of business that you can reasonably expect to generate as a result.

Once you have decided on the size of your ad, you will need to write the ad itself. In advertising this is known as the ad "copy". If you are looking for a simple all text ad to appear in the classifieds, the newspaper ad specialist can take your text over the phone or Internet and format the ad for you. If you are looking for a more complicated ad with graphics and fancy fonts you will need to hire a graphic artist or do the work yourself. A great place to find talented and inexpensive artists is often at you local art college. Many art students will be happy to have the exposure and experience to put in their portfolios. A simple flier will be enough to get some phone calls from this talent pool. You can also find local talented artists through Internet classifieds.

Before meeting with a graphic designer, think what you would like your ad to say. Draw out several possible sketches of your ad. Make sure to include your email or phone number. Hit all the points that you would on a cold call, but remember that newspapers generally charge by the word. Keep your message short, efficient, and effective. You will need to make sure that your graphic designer provides your ad in the form of a JPEG, PNG or PDF. These are computer file types that are specifically designed to contain images. Any qualified graphic designer will be familiar with these three file types. Once you have the ad in one of these file types, all you will need to do is to email the file to the newspaper. You can also walk a computer disc down to the newspaper. Email is the preferred method, however.

The yellow pages are another type of print advertising. Often, the companies that publish yellow pages also have yellow page websites as well. This means that you can tie in your yellow page ad with any website or online campaign.

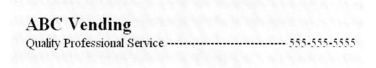

Figure 7.2 **A typical yellow page ad. In place of the address you can often place a positive message about your company.**

Yellow page ads have the same general style as newspaper ads. Opening any yellow page phone book will show you the similarities between these two media types. There are simple one line text adds that list only a name and phone number, and there are large half page all color ads. Again as with all advertising, the bigger the ad, the more it will cost. Ads can actually become rather expensive for a small business owner. To make it a little easier to advertise in the yellow pages these companies often offer monthly, quarterly or annual payment plans. You will need to do another cost benefit analysis that considers all the aspects of your particular situation.

One difference between yellow page advertising and newspaper advertising is that yellow pages are published much less frequently than newspapers. You will need to plan ahead a little more with yellow page ads than with newspapers. You will need to call the company or companies that publish in your area and find out when their deadlines are to publish in the upcoming edition. Your ad will need to be submitted and ready before this date. If you miss a deadline, plan to have your advertisement ready when the next one rolls around.

You may also wish to consider advertising in the smaller more targeted types of yellow pages. These often include foreign language editions (e.g. Spanish or Russian) and interest groups (e.g. Gay and Lesbian or Feminist). These types of publications often have lower costs and lower circulation. However, these options are worth considering.

Locating Services

If the methods that have been previously described are not to your liking, or too time consuming, you can use the services of a locater. A locater is a person or company whose entire business is finding locations for vending machine companies. They do all of the hard part of actually getting someone to say "yes" to receiving a vending machine from your company. Once they have found someone to say "yes" they call you and tell you the specifics of the location. These specifics should include the address, type of business, contact person, and phone number. Generally you can drive by the location and get a feel for it before you commit to buying it from the locating company. However, they prefer you do not approach the location until after you have paid their fee. Never pay in advance.

Once you have decided to purchase the location from the locating company, you will need to go by the new location and introduce yourself and do a site survey (the notion of a site survey will be discussed in the next chapter).

The easiest places to find a locating company are on the internet, or from another vending company or vending supplier. You do need to be aware that not all locating companies are created equally. Do your own research. Make sure that the company you have selected is one that has a long history and is one that can deliver what it has promised. Also make sure that the fees being charged by the company are in line with their competitors and are acceptable to the budget you have established for new locations.

Buying Existing Locations

Another option is to buy existing locations from other vending companies. Usually this is best accomplished by buying the vending machines that are already located at the site. If the machines are leased you will have to work to transfer all of the paperwork over to your company from the previous company.

There are usually two situations in which you can buy existing locations. The first is that a vending operator has decided to go out of business. The second situation is that a large competitor has decided to sell some of their locations.

A vending business that is going out of business can be shutting down for may reasons. The operator could be retiring, decided they have other priorities, could have a new baby, or have no time. They could also be going out of business because they have established a poor reputation and have mismanaged their accounts or have poor performing accounts. These last reasons are things to be aware of and fear. If you sense any of these problems, it is best to walk away from the deal. Don't let dreams of all the riches you can make cause you to buy a lemon location or a worthless machine. If it sounds too good to be true, it probably is.

Vending machines on location are far more valuable than vending machines in a mini-storage locker. When a vending operator goes out of business, they can often receive a much higher price for their machines while they are still making money.

Vending machines that are for sale on location can often be found in the local newspaper or from the local vending community. When buying these machines it is best to exercise caution to protect your investment. You will need to confirm that the machine is earning what the seller is advertising. Ask for any financial records that they might have. Inspect the insides of the machines to make sure that they are in good working condition. Try buying ten items from the machines and make sure the bill validators, motors, and displays all work.

The reasons that a large vending company might be selling machines are a little more elusive. Large vending companies make more money than small companies but often operate on smaller profit margins and have higher overhead costs. An example will help.

Imagine you are a small vending company. You are your only employee and you have ten machines. Each of your machines produces $500 a year in profit. It takes you two hours a week to service your route. Your costs to earn that $5000 annually are minimal. All you have to spend is money for the gas and the time it takes you to drive around town. You have no costs associated with employees such as worker's compensation insurance, human resource managers, or payroll costs.

This is not the case for a large vending machine company. It is not an exaggeration to say that it costs any company in America upwards of $500 a month just to have an employee. This does not take into account the employee's wages. Those are all the costs of insurance, management, and payroll taxes. This means that the larger vending companies require large volume vending machine locations for the accounts to be profitable after all these costs. Smaller accounts often do not generate enough profit to warrant an employee's time.

This creates an opportunity for a smaller, independent operator. A smaller operator can manage and profit from these smaller accounts that larger companies have no interest in. To find these locations simply try calling the larger companies and telling them what you are looking for. They may tell you that they do not sell accounts or they may be more than happy to talk to you. If you establish a positive relationship with the managers of these large vending companies, you may have found a consistent supply of good locations at fair prices.

One aspect that is often overlooked when buying a location is talking to the business manager. Make sure that they are aware of the potential change of ownership. Make sure that they approve of the change and have all of your contact information in the event of a problem. Ask if there have been any problems with the machines. Ask if they are happy with the service they have received so far. Assure them of both your professionalism and your reliability. This would be an excellent time to buy one of those pizza lunches for the office (if it is not too large) to establish a good relationship right away.

The only problem with buying machines from other vending operators is that they know the value of the machines that they own. Agree to a fair price but be cautious and don't let yourself be taken advantage of.

Conclusion

In this chapter several inexpensive and simple methods of finding new location for your business have been discussed. At this point you should:

- ✓ Decide on a monthly budget for your advertising.
- ✓ Write a direct mail letter for your company. You do not need to have letterhead or envelopes at this point. Just write the body of the letter.
- ✓ Find the contact information for the phone books and newspaper advertising departments in your area.
- ✓ Find 3 online advertising sites.
- ✓ Find 5 community bulletin boards.
- ✓ Design a business card.

8

Setting Up and Keeping Accounts

Once you have found a location lead, there are a number of steps that must be taken to turn that lead into a new location for your machines. These steps and some decisions that must be made before setting foot at a location are detailed in the following pages.

Initial Meeting and Site Survey

The first thing that you need to do when setting up a vending machine location, is meet the office manager and introduce yourself. The old adage of never getting a second chance at a first impression is especially true here. Make sure that you are well prepared and look professional. It is very important to convey the message that you will make their job easier and not become another problem in their daily routine.

You will need to discuss what types of machines they need. Ask how many employees they have and look around the office. Try to figure out how busy the office is. Decide what machine types would be the best fit for this location. Politely suggest these types to the manager and ask their opinion. If the office is only in need of tabletop machines, suggest these. If the office is going to need ten soda and snack machines, suggest those.

It is always a good idea to take pictures of the machines that you want to place and show them to the manager. Nothing will make your day more miserable than having placed a very heavy vending machine, and having the manager say they do not approve of the machine. Discuss what types of product the employees would like and see if they have any particular preference for one product line over the other. If you have decided to make use of contracts, this is the time to present the contract for review and approval. This would also be a great time to discuss commission rates and procedures. Ideally, these would be spelled out in any contract.

Once all the consulting is out of the way you will need to do a site survey. This is best done with the manager serving as your guide, but you can do it alone if they are busy.

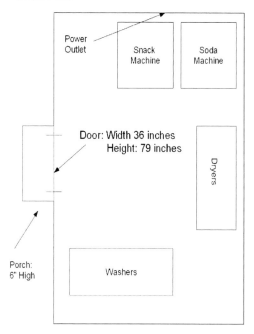

Figure 8.1 A detailed site survey along with pictures will allow you to communicate with movers where a machine will be placed as well as provide you with information about the location after you have left.

You have several goals during the site survey. You need to find a spot for your machines at the business location that has ALL of the following characteristics:

- The location is safe for your machines and the business.
- The location meets all of the electrical needs of your machines.
- The location is easily accessible to the employees and any relevant customers.
- It must be possible and hopefully simple to move your largest vending machine to this location.

When doing the site survey you will need a tape measure, pencil and paper. Draw a bird's eye view of the area around where the machine

105

will be placed. Measure the widths and heights of doors and hallways and make sure to write these numbers down. You need to make a map of the area that will help you or the people you hire to move the machines to the location safely, quickly, and efficiently. If you are hiring people to move your machines, make sure that the information on the map will be easily accessible to anyone, not just you. It is also a good idea to take pictures of the area from several angles for future reference.

Once your site survey is completed, say goodbye to the manager and let them now when the machines will be delivered. If you have a business card, make sure they have it. Remember, an important goal of this meeting and the survey is to assure the managers or business owners of your professionalism and ability to do what you have promised, as well as gathering necessary information.

Maintaining goodwill at your new location

Taking care of your machines on location is an essential skill to have in the vending industry. You need to learn to keep your accounts happy, protect your investment, and maximize your profits. This section will cover a variety of tips to achieve all of these goals.

Communication with account managers

Proper communication with account managers is absolutely essential to keeping your accounts. Never under any circumstances pop into an account, take out the money and restock the machine without also popping in on the manager (if they are out or busy talk to someone on staff or just give them a wave) to make sure that the machine is working and that there have not been any problems. Managers will tolerate a couple of problems over time, but if the machine becomes a problem that they have to actively manage and it adds to their workload, they will begin to look for another vending machine provider.

It is imperative that you make sure that a current phone number and contact information is clearly visible on the machine. This is best achieved with a sticker. An example of what your sticker should look like is:

This Machine is Owned and Operated by:
ABC Vending
123 Any Street
Any town USA 99999
(555)-555-5555

Please call in the event your product is not properly dispensed, or you are unhappy with your product in any way.

Use a shiny metallic or brightly colored sticker that is clearly visible and draws attention to itself. If unhappy customers are unsure of what to do they will go bug the manager or their staff. This must be avoided.

Refunds

You also need to have a plan to issue refunds in the event of unsuccessful vends or if customers are unhappy with your product. This plan should be made very clear to the account manager as well once the machines are delivered. They should not be left unsure of what to do and be forced to give refunds out of their own pocket.

How you deal with refunds is something for you to decide. You can drive out to every location in the event of a problem and personally hand someone a refund or proper product. You can be called and issue the refund by mail. Ultimately you just need to make sure that you have a plan and that everyone involved in the location is aware of it, especially the manager.

Freebies and goodwill

It is also never a waste of product to offer the manager or members of the staff free drinks when you show up. Ideally this would be product that is nearing but not over its expiration date. Instead of being wasted it is now being converted into goodwill, and goodwill is a commodity that can be very expensive to buy back once it is lost.

Free product needs to be thought through carefully, however. If you are buying a case of soda for the staff every time you show up, this can wreck your profit margin. If you stop once it has become customary you can be viewed as stingy. Start out gradually and maybe offer just the manager something periodically. Go from there. Remember, the goal is just to get them to like you. If you are already liked, don't offer anything. If your machine has ripped off a few office workers, give them each a free soda with their refunds.

Conclusion

By now you have a pretty good idea of the simple process of meeting with location managers and planning machine delivery. At this point you should undertake to:
- ✓ Decide on a plan for dealing with refunds.
- ✓ Design an identification sticker for your company. Maker sure that all of your contact information is on the sticker and is correct. A logo is nice but not essential.
- ✓ Draw up a form to use for site surveys.

9

Moving Your Machines Around

WARNING

Moving vending machines can be a dangerous procedure if not handled carefully. Follow all equipment manufacturers' instructions carefully after reading them thoroughly. Never exceed the printed maximum load capacities. Always have help when moving heavy loads. Never take any chances. Make sure all equipment is secure before attempting to move it. If you are unsure of safety, DO NOT PROCEDE. The author assumes no liability for any injury that may result from improper equipment use.

Simply put, vending machines are big, heavy, clunky pieces of equipment that are not especially designed for easy movement. This is a nice fact; when your machines are where you left them each time you arrive to service them. This is unpleasant when you have to place them.

To move vending machines you will need the appropriate equipment. This usually means a truck of some kind, and some moving equipment.

A truck is absolutely essential to moving a vending machine. The full size machines can weigh well over 700 pounds completely unloaded. A pickup truck will do but make sure that the engine has enough capacity and the towing limits are observed. A box truck designed for moving will do nicely. As will an open top trailer. This is often an easy proposition in that trailers are often lower to the ground and have built in ramps.

If you do not own a truck and the capital requirements of purchasing even a used truck are not something you want to deal with, you can rent a consumer moving truck. These are perfectly adequate to the needs of a vending machine company. All have ramps and you can request a lift gate as well. The costs of these are fairly reasonable and can include all of the necessary insurance under one fee.

Lift Gates

Lift gates, as were discussed in Chapter 6, are an almost essential piece of equipment when moving a heavy vending machine. While machines can be loaded onto a truck using a ramp, it is much easier to load the machine onto a lift gate and allow the hydraulics to do the rest of the work. Once the machine is level with the truck bed, it can then be moved into a position where it can be secured and moved safely.

Useful moving equipment

All of the types of equipment discussed in the following sections are fairly inexpensive. Even so these costs may be inconvenient for a small business. That being said, most of this equipment can be purchased even cheaper by keeping an eye on the classifieds in your local newspaper. In addition all of this equipment can be rented from equipment suppliers. The costs of this are fairly reasonable, but can add up quickly. If you expect to be moving a lot of machines, it is recommended that you seriously think about buying some used equipment.

Moving Hand Trucks

The vending machine mover's best and most reliable friend is the heavy duty appliance hand truck. This differs from a standard hand truck by the fact that the wheels are set closer to the blade to allow easy tipping of the load. In addition these hand trucks are of a heavier construction to address the much heavier load. Also, this type of hand truck has built in straps to secure the load before moving it. Always use a hand truck that has a sufficient load capacity to safely move the machine in question. Never exceed the maximum load capacity. Death and destruction can result!

Many heavy duty hand trucks are specifically designed to move vending machines. These have extra features such as fold out wheels that will help to support very cumbersome and heavy loads. An example of this type of equipment is the model WRV-60-EC from Wesco Industrial Products Incorporated (www.wescomfg.com). This unit features a 1200 lb. max load capacity, tie down straps, and retractable casters to support the load while it is being moved.

Figure 9.1 The Wesco WRV-60-EC is a hand truck suitable for moving vending machines. Picture used with permission of Wesco Industrial Products Inc.

Always have help moving machines. Extra people can be of enormous help when you cannot see around corners and when moving the machine. Remember, safety always comes first!

Pallet Jacks

Pallet jacks are especially useful when moving snack machines that sit on legs and have a clearance from the ground of several inches. Using a narrow pallet jack you can lift the entire machine and move it easily. Unfortunately, most soda machines do not have ground clearance and are best moved using the next type of equipment.

Pallet jacks are a very common type of equipment in warehouse operations. Pallet jacks are very similar, in principle, to forklifts. Using a hydraulic hand crank, an operator can lift very heavy loads and move it using the wheels on the pallet jack.

Figure 9.2 Pallet jacks are very useful when moving machines that have legs. The space between the machine bottom and the floor allows the tines of the fork to be slid underneath. Once in place the machine can be lifted using the jack, and slid using the wheels.

Rol-A-Lifts

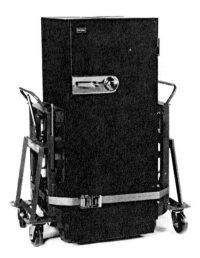

Figure 9.3 A Rol-A-Lift is an especially useful type of equipment. Placed on opposite sides of a vending machine, the wheels can be engaged to allow the machine to be rolled into position. Photo used with permission from Skarnes Incorporated.

A Rol-A-Lift is an extremely useful and versatile piece of moving equipment. These carts are used to move oddly shaped and oversize loads that would be hard to move otherwise. A Rol-A-Lift cart is actually a pair of two wheeled carts each with a hydraulic jack and optional straps. A pair of forks, similar to a pallet jack, is inserted underneath the load from each of the carts. Once both sets of forks have been inserted underneath the machine on opposite sides of the load, a hand operated hydraulic jack on each cart is engaged. This raises the machine off of the ground and leaves it on wheels to be easily rolled where it needs to go. Having this type of equipment is strongly recommended and will eliminate many headaches when moving a cumbersome vending machine.

Straps

There are other types of moving equipment out there that may be of use to you in a particular situation.

Ratcheting straps are very helpful to a vending machine mover. These are used to secure the load during transport. The ratcheting mechanism ensures a very snug fit for the machine and safety for the movers.

Figure 9.4 No move is complete without straps to hold the load in place. Never attempt to move a load without first securing it and never exceed the maximum load rating of the straps.

Never under any circumstances try to move a load without first properly securing it to the vehicle with these straps. Extreme damage can result from a very heavy vending machine suddenly tipping over during transport. In a situation like that, property damage lawsuits may be the very least of your headaches.

Also make sure that you adhere to the maximum load rating on the straps. Never under any circumstances exceed this rating!

Some helpful moving tips

Vending machines, as has already been stated, can be tricky to move. Here are presented several tips to make your life easier (and safer).

Some vending machines are wider than a standard door jam. These machines can be slipped through doorways by opening the vending machine's door and "swinging" the machine inside.

You can always lighten the load of a machine, and make it far less cumbersome by removing any shelves or other movable parts. This will also prevent these parts from knocking around and being damaged.

If your machine has a glass front, tape the glass to prevent shattering during transport. Broken glass everywhere is a headache no one needs.

When in doubt, there are professionals

As much fun as moving a vending machine sounds, some people are just not interested. In that case, you can hire professional movers to do the job for you.

You need to keep in mind when hiring agents to move the machines for you, that their professionalism is representative of your company. A highly unprofessional company can even cost you a location. If you do not feel this sense of professionalism from the moving company representative, you should probably choose a different company.

The easiest way to find a moving company is to use the phone book. You will need to have the specifications of the move that you are planning when calling the moving company. You will need to tell them what you have to be moved, and when you need to have it moved. You should know the approximate weight of the machine and its dimensions. You should be prepared to fax over the site survey diagrams of both where the machine is going and where it is currently located. You will need to give them all of your contact information, especially a phone number where you can be reached during the move. In the event of a problem you do not want movers trying to figure out what to do. This can give you a bad reputation with the business manager and the moving company.

You will also need to make arrangements to pay. Most moving companies will be reluctant to extend credit to a company that they have never dealt with. Most likely you will need to give them a credit card or pay in advance on a specified rate. You can also meet them at the job site and pay the movers directly. In the event that they do extend credit, make sure you pay them promptly and properly. As your business grows, you will have need of reliable movers, and they can sometimes be hard to find. Hold on to them once you have found them.

Once the machine has been delivered, get there as soon as possible to place a lock in the machine and fill it with product. Getting the machine up and running as quickly as possible will be a good demonstration of your company's professional attitude.

Conclusion

Hopefully, you were already familiar with some of the moving equipment listed in this section. If not you know have a basic idea of what it takes to move full size vending machines. To help with business planning you should now:

- ✓ Decide what type of equipment you would like to use to move vending machines. This will be based on the types of machines you plan to buy or already own.

- ✓ Look in the classifieds, online and at equipment retailers and determine the costs of purchasing this equipment either new or used.
- ✓ Call several equipment rental companies and find out what it will cost to rent the types of equipment that you need.
- ✓ Find several moving companies that will accept contracts to move vending machines.

10

Servicing Your Machines

Servicing your machines is probably the most important activity you will engage in once your machines are on location. This activity entails refilling your machines and collecting money. In addition you will also carry out inspections and routine cleaning of your machines.

Planning Your Route

If you have more than one location, you will generally want to service more than one location at a time. This is more efficient than servicing one machine at a time. The list of locations that you plan to service at one time is commonly referred to as a route.

Planning your route to be efficient will save you both time and money. Three considerations should be in your mind during the planning. These are geography, need of servicing, and timing. All three of these will be explained in the following paragraphs.

Geographic consideration should strongly influence how your route is organized. You will want to service locations that are close together at a similar time. This will keep the time that it takes you to service your route to a minimum and will keep your fuel expenses low as well. The first location should be the one farthest from your base. That way you will work your way home as the day progresses not farther away. You should plan which roads to take and avoid areas of known traffic congestion at those parts of the day. This will also make your job shorter and mean less time sitting in the car. Your back and posterior will thank you.

The need of servicing is another aspect that you need to consider when planning your route. It is entirely probable that all of your machines will not need restocking at the same time. This means that if you service all your machines at once you could be wasting your efforts. You may have two sets of machines on different service schedules. It is possible you will need to service one set weekly and both sets only biweekly.

It would be best to service only the locations that need your attention. To determine the need for servicing, start out on a set schedule. A weekly service plan is a good place to start. If your machines are constantly sold out when you arrive, begin servicing them more frequently. If nothing has been sold cut back to a biweekly plan. You will also need to take the seasons into account when planning your service schedule. In northern climates you will sell less soda in winter. In warm southern areas where cold winters are less common, your service schedule may be fairly constant. Use your best judgment and intuition to determine when to service your machines.

You also need to take timing into consideration. You obviously cannot service your machines when the business is closed. This means that you may only be able to service on weekdays. The managers at your location may prefer you service on a particular day or at a particular time. Many businesses prefer not to have their work or customer areas cluttered with your equipment during business hours. You also need to find a schedule that works with your personal and family responsibilities. If your children have soccer practice on Thursdays, you may find it difficult to service your machines on that day of the week.

Your Service Hand Truck

The most essential tool that you will need when servicing your machines, is a good, reliable hand truck. This is not an area to save a few pennies. Buy a sturdy unit with good wheels that you can rely on. You may also want to consider a hand truck that can be converted into a service cart as shown in the picture below. The hand truck shown in the follow picture is the model 156-S25-Z2, again from Wesco Industrial Products Incorporated (www.wescomfg.com). Featuring all-steel construction and rugged wheels this is an excellent choice that will serve you reliably for years. In addition to the rugged construction, this model features a 700 lb. max load capacity in two wheel mode and a 1000 lb. capacity in four wheel mode. These high load capacities will be very useful when hauling product between your machines and service vehicle.

It is worth noting that the hand trucks you will use to service your machines are not suited to move your machines. They will not have straps or sufficient load capacities.

Figure 10.1 This is the Wesco Manufacturing Inc. Model 156-S25-Z2. This hand truck can be used in either upright or four wheel mode depending on the particular job. This feature can be extremely useful.

When You First Arrive

When you first arrive at your location you will want to park somewhere that is convenient to the location's business activities and that will allow you to unload your product easily.

After you have parked and secured your vehicle and before you unlock your machines, you should pay a visit to the location manager. Keep it brief if they are busy. Your aim is to see how things have been going. If there have been problems with the machines they will let you know. The manager will also let you know if you need to stock more of one type of product or bring in a new one. These conversations can be invaluable in diagnosing malfunctions or increasing sales. They also go a long way towards maintaining a positive image for your business and keeping the relationship between you and the manager healthy.

Servicing Your Machines

After you have parked your vehicle and talked to the manager it is time to service your machines. Before filling them with product and removing the money, it is a good idea to take a look at the machines. Make sure that the locking devices are intact and have not been tampered with. Make sure that there is no graffiti on the machine. Basically, make sure the machine exterior is in good shape and looking professional.

Figure 10.2 Bulk machines are filled by removing the tops of the machines and simply pouring in more product. The automatically takes care of the need for product rotation.

Once the exterior of the machine has been inspected you may move on to stocking the machine and removing the money. If you are working on a bulk machine, open the product compartment, usually done by unlocking the top of the machine. To stock a full size machine, you will need to open the door.

To actually stock the machine you need to put more product in the machine, paying attention to product rotation. Product rotation is the system by which the oldest product is used first. In a bulk machine this is done by gravity. The product is dispensed from the bottom of the machine and filled from the top. This means the candy that will expire soonest (but hasn't already) is always at the bottom ready to be sold first.

Soda machines without a glass fronts are stocked in a similar way. They are filled from the top and dispensed from the bottom. This again means that the product that will pass (but has not) its expiration date first will be sold first.

Figure 10.3 Soda machines are often stocked from the top down. This means the oldest soda will always be sold first before it expires.

Soda machines that do have a glass front and snack machines employ a shelf system. The oldest product is always in the front and new product is placed in back. As product is sold the newer items move forward. When adding new product, make sure that you are placing it behind any existing inventory to ensure freshness.

Figure 10.4 Snack machines and glass front soda machines are stocked front to back. As product is sold new product moves forward.

When filling your machines with product try to fill the selections to capacity. This will make sure that the chances of all product selections being available between servicing are greatly increased. This also diminishes the chances of you losing sales due to lack of selection. You should also pay attention to the sold out items. If a particular selection is sold out each week, you may need to consider devoting additional selections to that item. This will also help maximize your sales. Lastly, you should check the expiration dates of the product in your machine. If anything has expired, remove it from your machine and add it to your waste sheet. These are discussed in Chapter 11. You do not want expired product reaching your customers!

Removing Money and Adding Change

You will need to remove the cash from your machines when you service them. This is a fairly straightforward proposition but a few words are warranted.

Money in bulk vending machines will be all coin. These will be in a single coin box in the bottom and usually the back of the machine. There is no need for change in a bulk machine so just take it all. With full size machines, it is only slightly more complicated.

Figure 10.5 The above picture shows the bill validators, coin mechanisms and coin boxes (beneath the coin mechanism) of a snack and soda machine.

The money in a full size vending machine will be in three places. Bills will be in the bill validator and coins will be located in both the coin mechanism and the coin box. You can remove all of the bills from the validator and take them with you. Next, look in the coin box. Only extra coins that are not needed to make change are dropped into the coin box. If the box is empty, it means that the coin tubes in the coin mechanism are not full. You should always leave these full and if necessary, bring change with you to fill them. Only take coins from the coin box. If you have a change machine at the location, you should also fill the coin reserve in that as well.

Since it would be impractical to count the money from each machine while you are still servicing your route, you need to keep the money from each machine separate from others. You can easily do this with cash bags like those shown in Figure 10.5 or you can even use plastic sandwich bags.

You also need to keep the money safe during your route. You can do this by keeping a low profile while servicing your machines, installing a safe in your service vehicle, or even swinging by the office after each visit. This last solution is impractical but can be used as a last resort.

Figure 10.6 Bank bags can be very useful in keeping money from different machines separate.

Cleaning Your Machines

In your vehicle you should have some all purpose cleaner. Each time you service a machine you should take a few seconds to remove any fingerprints, grease smudges, soda or candy messes, graffiti or dust. Doing this will keep your machines looking professional and sanitary. This will help keep your company in the good graces of the location's manager and your customers. No one will buy food products from a machine that looks unsanitary.

You should also clean the bill validator using a specially sized alcohol pad periodically. These are sold by most vending machine suppliers. Proper cleaning will make sure that the electronic eye will not reject bills unnecessarily.

Inspecting and Testing Your Machines

While conversations with management can alert you to any problems that may have occurred since your last visit, they may not do so. To make sure that your machines are working properly you should inspect and test them before leaving.

Inspecting your machine is easy. Make sure there are no jams in the coin slot or bill validator and make sure that the product slot is free from obstruction.

Testing your machine usually means putting some money in them and making sure that the product and correct change are dispensed quickly and efficiently. With a bulk machine try five vends and make sure you get everything you should and the coin is safely deposited in the box. With a full size soda machine (that does not have a glass front) buy a soda from each selection. Try this with both bills and coin to make sure the validator and coin mechanism are both working.

With glass front machines such as snack machines and glass front soda dispensers, test vend one item from each shelf. Again use coins and bills to make sure both money components are in good working order.

Conclusion

Servicing machines can be one of the most rewarding aspects of operating a vending machine route. After all, this is the point when you get to collect all the money! To help your business planning it would be helpful to:

- ✓ Go shopping and compare prices on service hand trucks. Look for units that can be converted to carts as well.
- ✓ Put together a list of all the cleaning supplies that you will need to keep your machines looking professional.
- ✓ Plan how you will keep money from each machine separate and how you will keep it safe while you service the route.

11

Inventory Management

Making sure that your machines are stocked is one of the most important aspects of managing your business. If your machines are empty, that means sales are walking away and customers are getting the impression that they cannot rely on you or your machines to provide them with the products they want. The questions are, where do you get your products and how do you best store and deliver them to your customers?

Where to buy your product

In the vending business, it is usually easiest to buy your soda from the local bottler. They almost always have the best prices, availability and will usually deliver the product right to your storage facilities. Bottlers generally have a minimum order of around 10 cases (24 individual cans or bottles per case). They are often willing to offer credit to your company (provided you qualify) or can conduct business on a cash on delivery basis. Usually you will be scheduled for delivery on specific days of the week. You will have a specific deadline to call in your order. It is often difficult to get product other than your scheduled delivery days. As such, you will need to do some planning ahead before you order.

The easiest, although not the cheapest, way to buy your non-soda product is from a local wholesale "big box" store or from a bulk grocery store. (If you are supplying can machines you can buy those at wholesale clubs as well. Twenty ounce bottles are often hard to come by from anyone other source than the bottler at wholesale prices.) You will often be required to pay a membership fee to shop at these stores. The costs of these fees are small and generally tax deductible. These establishments allow you to buy at wholesale prices that are close to those offered by specialized wholesale distributors. Their selection is fairly good and you will be able to stock a full size snack machine with little if any redundancy in selection. The downside to this supply method is that you generally pay a little higher price than that offered by vending specific wholesalers. The profits from items purchased from wholesale clubs are still very high but you are giving up a little money. In addition, their selection can rarely if ever compare to specialized distributors. What happens in the event that you need a beef jerky product and your local wholesale club doesn't have a prepackaged item that fits that description?

Another concern with the wholesale club solution is that they do not stock the same levels of product that a specialized distributor does. You can often encounter empty shelves and supply interruptions. While this may not seem like a huge problem, an account manager without his favorite snack for two weeks can cause you to lose an account.

To solve that problem it is often advantageous to buy your product through a specialized vending distributor. These companies often offer competitive pricing, have the best variety of products and rarely have empty shelves. Their business is to ensure they have supplies for you to buy and stock your machines with. These suppliers can often be found on the Internet or through a local phone directory. It is preferable that this supplier be located in the same city as you to avoid all the problems involved in shipping product (i.e. shipping costs and product spoilage).

In the event that your town or city does not have a vending specific wholesale distributor, there is a very good chance that there is a distributor that supplies the convenience stores in your area. These will make an excellent substitute and should be able to supply your new business with everything it needs. These companies can be found using the same techniques as described above.

Product Freshness and Preservation

Many of the products that you will be selling have expiration dates. These need to be religiously adhered to. Ignoring these dates and stocking your machines with product of low quality can cost you much more in the long run than the loss of some product. A simple rule is that if you suspect the quality of your supplies, do not stock them.

Another important factor to consider is that many of the items that you stock will be sensitive to heat. This can cause a bit of a problem in the high summer months. At that time temperatures can often reach 100 degrees and, unless you are using a refrigerated snack machine, your machines do not have air conditioning. This means that if the location itself is not air conditioned you cannot stock anything that melts. This means almost no candy whatsoever. In those cases it is best to discuss the problem with the account manager. Few of them will want melted products in their machines, and a little honesty goes a long way. You can either move the machine somewhere that is air conditioned or you can stock products that are less sensitive to heat such as chips, nuts, pretzels and baked goods with long shelf lives.

Storing your product and equipment

Your business is going to need a place to store its equipment and extra product. Four of the most common solutions are discussed in detail in the following pages.

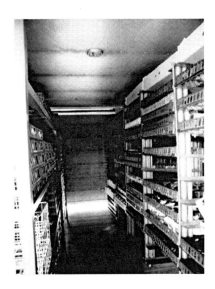

Figure 11.1 Using your vehicle as your storage area offers many advantages but also brings risk.

In the vehicle

By far the simplest solution to storage is to keep everything your business needs inside of your primary service vehicle. Storage in your vehicle means that everything is self contained and mobile. The only other thing you need is a parking space. This means that even if you are renting an apartment you can conveniently store everything in your assigned space. The downside to this is that inside your service vehicle is not a climate controlled environment. This being the case it can get very hot inside during the summer and cold in the winter. This can lead to product spoilage in both cases. Your vehicle is also not the most secure location in the world. Vehicle break-ins are common and a fully loaded service vehicle is a very tempting target.

Using your primary residence

After storing everything in the service vehicle, the next easiest solution to storage is to use your primary residence. This solution offers the advantages of climate control to prevent product spoilage, along with convenience and added security. The downside is that this could be considered commingling and could expose your personal assets to liability. You should discuss this possibility with your attorney prior to storage at your primary residence.

Renting a mini storage locker

A mini storage locker is a simple and relatively cost effective solution to storing your product and equipment. These units are available in a variety of sizes from a 5'x5' unit all the way to a 25'x25'. Cost for these units range from $25 to $500 a month. This solution offers convenience, as these storage facilities are available in any part of any city and can easily be found near your home. As was previously stated, they are relatively low cost when compared to professional warehouse space and will not strain your budget. Most do not, however, offer any form of climate control and product spoilage due to excessive heat and cold should be considered. Climate controlled units are available, but they are a little more rare and may require a little homework to find. These will eliminate the threat of product spoilage and should be strongly considered.

Additionally, storage unit parks offer a relatively good level of security. Often you will find fenced and gated premises that are monitored by security cameras. Keypad entry systems are also very common.

Professional Warehouse Facilities

Professional warehouse facilities are companies that provide warehouse services for larger commercial customers. These are climate controlled environments that protect your investment. There are two types of these facilities. One type rents space similar to the mini storage arrangement. The other type provides all of the warehousing services. For a fee, they will store your merchandise by the pallet load. This is an outsourced warehouse management system and is unsuitable to the beginning vendor

Necessary Warehouse Equipment

If you decide to set up a warehouse, you will need to set it up to run properly and to protect your investment. The first thing that you need in a warehouse is shelves. You will need a lot of these. These are used to maximize the space that you have at your disposal, and to protect your product from spoilage. There are many options for shelving and the best place to look for these is at a store fixture or warehouse supplier. These can be found in your city or state, by looking in the yellow pages. These companies will happily mail you a catalog of all the latest and greatest products that they offer. Another good place to look is online classifieds and auctions. You can find good deals at these websites as well. Look for something local. Remember, these are sturdy metal shelves and will cost quite a bit to ship, so look locally first. You will want high capacity steel and particle board construction with a minimum distance of 3" between the floor and the lowest shelf. This will help prevent spoilage and molding in the event of water leakage.

In addition to shelving you may also have need for pallet jacks (if you are receiving pallet sized loads) and hand trucks to move the product around your space. A garbage can and recycling bin will also be useful as you will have a fair amount of plastic packaging and cardboard boxes.

You will also need to make sure that your warehouse facilities are strongly locked. Buy the strongest lock that money can buy. Your warehouse contains a good deal of capital investment and needs to be strongly protected. A combination lock will be helpful to allow delivery drivers to enter when you are not there, but may create a security risk.

Lastly, you will need a place to have delivery drivers place your invoices in the event that you are not there for delivery. This will help greatly in keeping your bills and receipts organized for cost analysis and tax time.

Figure 11.2 Raised shelving to prevent spoilage and pallet jacks to move supplies can be very helpful in your warehouse.

Inventory Management

Par Levels

Managing your inventory is an extremely important part of your office activities. Only through effective inventory management, can you control spending, track customer preferences, and predict future needs and sales.

To someone who has never managed an inventory it can at first seem a daunting task, however, with a little patience and discipline it can become very simple. Essentially, all you need to do is figure out how much you have of a particular item and how much you need. Once you have this information you can make educated decisions regarding ordering and budgeting.

This is accomplished by setting a number called a "par". This is the minimum of an item that you need to have in stock, below which you will need to order more. An example will help clarify this.

Item	**Par**	**In Inventory**	**Order**	**Supplier**
Candy Bar	2 Cases 36 Ct.	2 Cases	0 Cases	ABC Candy
12 oz. Soda	2 Cases 24 Ct.	1 Case	1 Case	Soda Bottler
20 oz. Soda	2 Cases 24 Ct.	0 Cases	2 Cases	Soda Bottler
Chips	1 Case 50 Ct.	0 Cases	1 Case	XYZ Vending

Figure 11.3 A par sheet is used in ordering. This sheet shows that one case of 12 oz. soda needs to be ordered along with two of 20 oz. soda and one case of chips. The sheet also shows that two cases of candy bars are in inventory.

Every week you sell 100 20 oz. bottles of a particular type of soda. This means that every week your inventory will be reduced by 100 bottles of soda. However, to save costs you buy in a pallet sized load of 1000 bottles. This means once you receive a delivery you have much more soda than you will need for the next couple of months. You will not need to order more of this soda until you get low. You decide that you will not order another pallet of this soda until you only have 200 bottles in stock. This allows a little cushion in the event that the bottler is out of stock temporarily. This number of 200 bottles is now your "par".

At first you will need to estimate pars for every item you have decided to carry. A good rule of thumb is to be sure that you have enough in inventory to fill every slot of every machine that you operate. This will make sure that your machines are filled and customers are satisfied. As you learn the preferences of the customers in your area and at your locations, you can adjust these numbers. You can also add or discontinue products as you deem it necessary. Always be flexible in your inventory. If one of your locations requests that you carry beef jerky where you had not before, do your best to satisfy this request in a cost effective and timely manner.

Ordering

Ordering will need to be carried out weekly. Most distributors and bottlers will set specific days of the week for you to call in your order for delivery later in the week. You will need to have this information when they ask you to provide it. These days are often inflexible. If you miss one of your order days, you will have to wait until next week. Some suppliers will allow you to do a "will call". This is when you go to their warehouse and pick up the supplies instead of having them delivered. Do not rely on this practice to keep your warehouse full. Some companies will allow this and others will flatly refuse.

You will need to make arrangements to have the product delivered. You will need to provide your supplier with the address to your warehouse and any addition details, such as which building it goes in, lock combinations or where they can get the key, etc. Do not expect the delivery people to place your items neatly on the shelves where you want them. The product will be left on a pallet on the floor and you will need to ensure you have received everything you ordered and organize it in your warehouse system. Compare what you receive carefully against your invoices.

Route Reports

Tracking your item sales will be a very useful tool in your inventory management scheme as well. You need to be intimately familiar with what items your customers like and buy repeatedly to properly maximize your profit potential. The easiest way to do this is to fill every slot in every machine each week. Then when you return to service the machine you will be able to see how many of each item has sold simply by counting. This information can then be recorded on a route report sheet and taken back to the office. You will also be able to quickly determine which items need to have additional selections devoted to them, and which items need to be discontinued.

Using a simple word processor or spreadsheet program you can generate a route report that can be modified as needed. Below you will find an example of a report. This is an only an example and can be supplemented as the needs of your business dictate.

Account Name:_____
Address:_____
Phone:_____ **Contact Name:**_____

	Week 1	Week 2	Week 3	Week 4
Item 1				
Item 2				
Item 3				
Item 4				
Item 5				
Item 5				
Item 7				
Item 8				
Item 9				
Item 10				

Money Collected:_____ _____ _____ _____

<u>**Figure 11.4**</u> **This is a simplified example of a route report format that could be used to track sales and revenues over a monthly period. In the rows for each item, one would track how many of each item is placed in the machine each week. You could also track how many of each item is sold each week. At the end of one month, the report is filed and another is prepared.**

<u>Expiration Dates, Spoilage and Waste Tracking</u>

In the event that items have reached their expiration date or have melted or otherwise spoiled, remove them from the machine or warehouse immediately. You do not want these being sold to customers. You will need to account for these items on what is termed a "waste sheet". This sheet will help you track the amount of product that was lost to spoilage. These items will need to be accounted for and replaced in inventory.

You will also be able to determine what types of items are susceptible to spoilage and how they were lost. Armed with this information, you can help to keep product waste low.

Inventory Tracking Systems

There are three convenient ways to track your inventory. The first is with a good old fashioned pen and paper on a convenient form of your own creation, or a columnar pad available at any office supply store. This is the simplest and cheapest by far. These can also be used to track item sales and wasted items as well.

	Item	**Amount Wasted**	**Reason for Waste**	**Cost**
1	Candy Bar	1 Dozen	Melted	$6.99
2	Soda	3 12 oz Cans	Passed Exp. Date	$1.50
3	Chips	1 2 oz Bag	Punctured Bag	$.45

Figure 11.5 A simple waste sheet following the format shown above can help you keep track of lost product and help you eliminate the causes for waste.

If you are one of those people who likes everything computerized, then the next simplest method of tracking your inventory is with a spreadsheet system. There are many of these types of programs available. They range in cost from free (OpenOffice Suite http://www.openoffice.org) to a few hundred dollars. They are easy to learn and use with any of the many available guide books and online tutorials.

The last option for tracking inventory is through one of the commercial software applications specifically designed for the vending industry. These offer very simple and straight forward user interfaces that take all of the guess work out of managing your vending business. They all have inventory management and route report options as well as other useful features. These are available online for a few hundred dollars and are often worth the tax deductible costs.

Conclusion

Controlling your costs and protecting your investment through proper and effective inventory management is an essential skill in building your vending business. The advice contained in this chapter will provide an excellent place to start in constructing an effective strategy.

To continue building your business plan and gathering information you should:

- ✓ Locate several mini storage locations near where you plan to do business. Find out how much they charge for their lockers.
- ✓ Locate and make contact with as many suppliers as you can. Obtain pricing and delivery information. It would also be a good idea to explore credit options at this time.
- ✓ Using whatever method you are most comfortable with, construct a "Par Sheet", "Waste Sheet", and "Route Report". Treat these as master copies that you can easily reproduce.

12

Protecting and Maintaining Your Machines

Protecting Your Investment

If you own the machines that you are operating, these represent a large capital investment for your business. If you are leasing the machines that you are operating, the last thing you need is a bill for damage to the machines. Machines that are not working properly are like a store that is closed. This can cost you sales and customers. All of these problems are addressed in this chapter. Here we will discuss ideas to protect your machines from theft and vandalism and methods to keep your machines working properly to make you money.

Machine Security

Everyone out there knows that vending machines contain tasty products and cold hard cash. However, unlike a convenience store with an attendant to watch the goods and cash register, or to call the police, your little stores are unattended. This means that only the automatic security features are in place to protect you investments and as such, require your attention.

Location, Location, Location

The first line of defense in protecting your machines against theft and vandalism is the machine's location. As was briefly mentioned when discussing the site survey, you need to make sure that where the machine is located will be safe. Ask yourself the following question:

- Is this area open 24 hours a day?
- Is this location in a good neighborhood?
- What security features does the business already provide?
- Does the location have security cameras?
- Is the location visible at night to the neighborhood or street?
- Is the area lit at night?
- Is the location isolated and away from plain sight?

The sheer size of full size machines will help make sure that they do not disappear one day. However, bulk candy machines should never be left out in the open 24 hours a day. Their small size will just about ensure that they will disappear during the night.

Ultimately, you decide where to put your machine, but know the answer to all of these questions beforehand. It is wise to drive by the location at night before doing the site survey so you know what things look like at night as well. This will help you decide where a safe location is when placing the machine.

Locks

After you have located the machine, there is nothing more important to protecting your machine than locks. Now for clarity in our discussion, we need to make a distinction between locks and locking mechanisms. Locks are mechanical devices that release upon the use of a key. Locking mechanisms are simple machines such as a screw-in door handle or a pop out latch that are used in conjunction with a lock to prevent the machines opening.

Figure 12.1 Bulk vending machines are often secured by cam locks like this one. The arm on the left prevent the access panel and coin box from opening.

Mechanical vending machines such as bulk candy and condom machines utilize what is called a "cam lock". A cam lock is a simple key lock that has a rotating metal latch that prevents the opening of the candy compartment or cash box. It is entirely possible that a machine may have more than one lock on it. These should be keyed alike for simplicity.

Cam locks use a latch system to prevent opening. They do not offer very much protection as a determined criminal will have little trouble breaking into the machine simply by prying. As such, mechanical machines should always be in open areas that are well lit and offer little chance of privacy. Twenty four hour access is also not recommended.

Another type of locking scheme that occurs less frequently on mechanical machines is a rod that goes through a series of metal loops on the door and machine superstructure. This prevents opening as long as the rod is intact. In addition to the rod, a supplemental hardened padlock should always be used.

Most modern full size vending machines employ a screw-in "T-handle". Some older machines utilize a pop out latch that releases the door.

Figure 12.2 A T-Handle secures the door of a full size machine closed by using the screw mechanism seen at the end of its long shaft. A plug lock prevents the handle from turning and unscrewing the door.

Both of these types of door handles require the use of a type of lock known as a plug lock. Plug locks come in many different security levels. You can get a simple bargain basement plug lock online for a couple of dollars. These locks will be made of soft brass. These can easily be opened with a good drill bit or even picked! If you have a machine in a well lit, highly visible, indoor 9AM-5PM location, one of these locks will do nicely. It is difficult to imagine no one mentioning the man with the electric drill in the middle of the car dealership showroom. However, these locks are inappropriate in all but the most secure locations.

Figure 12.3 Plug locks are very frequently used in the vending industry. These are used to secure T-handles and in combination with other lock systems.

For locations where there exists a risk of tampering, you will need to use a more secure and more expensive lock. Locks are not a place to be stingy with your money. A few dollars saved on a lock can cost you hundreds if not thousands in theft and vandalism. Medeco (medeco.com) and LAI (laigroup.com) are two companies that sell locks specifically designed for the vending industry. Many of their locks employ sophisticated key systems designed to eliminate the possibility of picking. In addition, their vending machine locks employ hardened cylinders which are very difficult if not impossible to drill. This does cause a problem in the event that you lose the key, however. In that event a locksmith will be forced to grind out the lock. Make sure you always have a back up key! A qualified locksmith that deals in locks of these types can supply you with as many locks as you need all keyed alike.

A sturdy hardened plug lock can do quite a bit to ensure that your machine is protected. Unfortunately, sometimes even this is not enough. In situations like that you can further reinforce your machine security by utilizing hasps and hidden shackle padlocks, commonly called "puck" locks. A hasp is a strong latch that is installed on the outside of the machine. For strength the hasp is bolted into the superstructure of the machine. For ultra high security you can install multiple hasps and hasps that cover the plug lock and t-handle as well. How discouraging will it be to a burglar after an hour of drilling a lock, to open it and find another hardened lock?

Figure 12.4 At less secure locations, shrouded hasps and hidden shackle padlocks can greatly enhance your security. Photo courtesy of Master Lock Company.

Beyond locks there are steps that can be taken to protect your machines. The first of these is conducting your business in a manner that makes your machine unappealing to a thief. The first of these is the placement of sticker or piece of paper that declares the money is removed from the machine daily. Even if this is not true it can be discouraging to a thief.

ATTENTION
All money removed from this machine daily.

You can also place stickers or fliers that advises a reward for information leading to the arrest of thieves of vandals.

Another good idea is to make use of the fear of video surveillance to help protect your machines. You can place stickers that advise that the machine is under surveillance. An example is:

SMILE!
YOU ARE ON CAMERA

Fake security cameras can be purchased to help with this illusion. These can be found online or at electronic stores and at very reasonable prices.

There also exist alarms that you can add to your machines. The simplest of these are so called "Tip Alarms". These alarms are activated when the machine is tipped to an angle that you specify (usually 10-45 degrees). When the machine is returned to an upright position the alarm deactivates. These alarms are powered using a simple 9-volt or 12-volt batteries and are very simple to install. It is recommended to use a model that utilizes a commonly available battery. 12-volt batteries are expensive and not as easily obtained as 9-volt batteries, using the 9-volts can help to simplify your business and save you money. More sophisticated alarms have door sensors and arming switches as well.

These alarms are not very expensive and are simple to operate. However, they do pose a problem. All of us hate to hear a car alarm mistakenly going off in the night, and the manager of one of your locations may not care for your alarm going off mistakenly, or going off uncontrollably in the event of a break in. Make use of the communication skills mentioned in previous pages to eliminate these potential problems right away. If security problems have arisen, discuss these problems with the account manager. Discuss your ideas to solve these problems and solicit the manager's advice as well.

Security Cages

Sometimes locks and hasps are just not enough to keep a machine secure. In these cases a security cage may be all that is left to enhance the security features of your machines. Security cages are large steel cages not unlike the types people use when swimming with sharks. They offer sturdy steel construction to protect your machine from break-ins but will allow customers freedom to use the machines. These can be a little expensive but will secure your machines to the maximum level of protection.

Figure 12.5 Like a shark cage, a vending machine cage offers a very high level of security. The cage must be breached before any attempt at the lock can be made.

Maintaining Your Equipment

After first ensuring the security of your machines, you will need to make sure they are kept in good working order. This is very important. Constantly malfunctioning equipment will quickly become a bother to managers and customers alike, and can ultimately cost you a location and money. In addition you will need to keep your machines attractive and professional looking.

Read The Manuals

Owning and reading the manuals for each type of machine you own, may seem obvious, but it is often overlooked. You can download these manuals from the internet rather easily. These are most often available as a PDF and will require a PDF reader. Reading the manual will familiarize you with your equipment and its operation. You will learn how to configure any onboard computers, and relevant error codes. This information can be invaluable in determining the cause of any malfunctions. One very useful additional section in most manuals will be a step by step troubleshooting guide. This can point you in the right direction in the event of a problem, and provided you cannot solve the problem, will allow you to convey more information to help a repair service technician.

Minor Repairs You can Do Yourself

Machines are going to malfunction and parts are going to break. These are facts of life. However, just like a car, simple preventative maintenance can save you many dollars and headaches in the long run.

Mechanical machines are simple reliable mechanisms to operate. Treated properly these machines can offer many years of reliable service. You should test vend each machine each time it is serviced to make sure it is working however. If a part does break in a mechanical coin mechanism, it is often far simpler to replace the whole mechanism rather than the individual part.

Full size electronic vending machines, are by their nature more complicated than the smaller mechanical vending machines. This means that there are more things to check and maintain on a full size machine. The main areas of concern are the bill validator, the coin mechanism, and the motors. Inspecting these each time and cleaning as necessary can save you a lot of grief and money.

Bill validators need to be cleaned periodically. To do this, you need to use a specially sized alcohol pad. This pad is inserted into the validator like a dollar would be. This removes all of the dirt and grime that builds up from the money. You should also check to make sure that there are no bills stuck inside the actual validator. Run a couple of dollars through just to make sure that everything is working properly.

The main problem that plagues coin mechanisms is jams. Unfortunately, many people think it's amusing to put anything into a vending machine coin slot. Just because something will go through the coin slot, does not mean it will go through the coin mechanism. Many odd things have been found jammed in a coin mechanism from quarters with attached strings, to Mexican pesos and other foreign coins, to gold jewelry!

Once a jam is in place, every coin that is inserted into the machine will get caught in the coin mechanism and increase the size of the jam. If this is not dealt with right away, the machine will keep accepting money and not vending any product. This will anger customers. To clear a jam, all you really need to do is remove the coin mech and clean it out. Usually just tipping it upside down will do the majority of the work. Make sure that you run a number of coins through the mechanism to make sure that everything is working before you leave. One little dime stuck somewhere can easily restart the jam.

Another feature that is offered on modern computerized vending machines is a mode that test vends each product. This is a good thing to do each and every time you service the machines. This will not only test all of the motors and prevent misvends, but will also make sure that product delivery paths are clear as well.

One system in full size vending machine that most operators should avoid attempting to fix is the refrigeration system. These systems are complicated to repair and are technical in nature and a simple mistake from lack of proper training can be quite costly. In addition the coolants used in these systems can require specialized handling that a lay person will be unprepared to provide.

In the event that you encounter a problem that is beyond your ability to fix, you can call a vending machine repair technician. If the machine is not working, make sure to hang an "Out of Order" sign on the machine and communicate with the location manager. Make sure to tell them that the machine is out of commission and what is wrong with it (try not to be too technical); at the same time you should tell them when the machine will be repaired.

There are four ways to find a repair technician. The first method provided you are using leased machines, is to contact your soda bottler. Bottlers maintain a staff of technicians to take care of all the machines that they have in the field. Your responsibilities concerning machine repair should have been spelled out in any agreements that you signed. These technicians usually will be able to service your machine in a couple of days. They are mobile and can service your machine in the field, but may require delivery of the machine for major repairs.

The second place to find a vending machine repair technician is from your local vending machine distributor. In addition to new machine sales, these businesses often offer machine upgrades and repairs as well. Usually they can service your machine in the field, but may require the machine to be delivered to them for major repairs, such as a new door.

The third place to find repair services are other vending machine companies. Large vending machine companies also maintain repair staff and it is possible that these can be hired to repair your machines. Also some people who have retired from the vending industry maintain a vending machine repair service. These people can usually be found only by word of mouth advertising.

The final place to find a qualified vending technician is in your mirror. Looking on the internet for "Vending Machine Repair Course" will yield many links to many reputable training programs. Look for one that appeals to you and complete the course. There will be a fee, but this might be the best option of all. This will eliminate the labor costs associated with having your machine repaired. In addition you can also possibly generate another income stream by offering repair services to other vending machine companies.

Break-Ins

A break-in can be one of the most discouraging and costly problems that can occur. It can be very demoralizing to come up to your machine to see broken glass and drilled locks. First and foremost make sure that the scene is safe and you are in no danger. Secondly, inspect the machine and secure whatever product, money, and parts that may be exposed. If it can be removed from the machine, remove it and secure it until such time as the machine is repaired and secure. It can be hard to understand the mind of a criminal but it is not uncommon for them to steal useless parts to sell for scrap metal or just to be cruel.

Once your machine is secured, you will need to call the police and file a police report. Realistically this will do little to recover your property or money, but is necessary if you are filing insurance claims and may be useful come tax time.

Once the police have left you will need to go about the business of repairing your machine. If all you need to do is put in a new lock or tighten a few bolts then do so on site. If the repairs are more complicated and require service personnel or even removal of the machine for a complete overhaul, speak to them manager about the situation. Let them know about arriving service people or the timetable for when the machine will be returned. Ideally, provided the machine needs to be removed, you should replace it at that time with a different machine. Managers can get impatient quickly and not replacing the machine can easily cost you an account if you are not careful.

Unsuccessfully Drilled Locks

A problem that can occur that is similar to a break in, is an unsuccessfully drilled lock. This can be infuriating because you will not be able to open your machine. In addition it is possible that the perpetrator will return to finish what they started.

The best thing to do in this situation is to place an additional lock on the machine in the event that a hasp lock is present, or failing that, have an emergency locksmith come to the site to drill or even grind out the lock. This will be an expensive repair but think what will happen if the machine, which is presumably filled with money and product, is opened and cleaned out.

Vandalism

It is a sad fact of life that people decide to vandalize the private property of others. Fortunately it is a relatively simple matter to undo the damage, most of the time.

In the event that a permanent marker has been used all you need to do is apply a soft vinyl scrubber and some paint thinner. This will not damage the paint and will remove the marker. This approach will often work when removing paint as well. You can also use an abrasive metal scrubber. This will work a little better but will scuff up the paint on your machine as well. One thing to note is to never use an abrasive metal scrubber on any of the plastic surfaces of your machine. This will irrevocably scratch up the plastic surfaces and lower the machines value and can ruin its professional appearance.

Coordinating A Repair

Coordinating a repair on one of your machines will be very similar to coordinating a vending machine move. Make sure that you know when the machine is to be repaired, and communicate this to the manager of the machine location. If you are not going to meet the technician during the repair (being present is recommended), you will need to make sure that the technician has a map of the location and a means of getting into the machine.

It is not recommended, but you can always leave a key hidden somewhere on the machine in a magnetic key holder. If you choose this option, make sure you have a spare and have the technician leave the key inside the machine when they are done. The coin box makes an excellent place to leave the key when they are finished.

Keeping Your Machines Looking Professional

Keeping your machines looking professional is an important responsibility. You need to make sure that your machines compliment the business locations where they reside. If your machines are dirty and unprofessional looking, they convey a bad message from you and the location and may upset business owners and customers alike.

Keeping your machines looking professional is really all about cleaning. To do this you need to keep a cleaning kit inside of the machines on location (most machines have compartments suitable for storage) or in your service vehicle. This kit should include:

- Glass cleaner

- All-purpose cleaner in a spray bottle
- Paper Towels
- Razor blade (good for graffiti)
- WD-40
- Q-tips
- Alcohol pads for cleaning the bill validator

Each time you service your machines, inspect them for grime or graffiti and make use of the cleaning kit as needed. Keep them looking as clean as possible.

Conclusion

Planning to protect your machines and knowing how to have problems fixed, is an important part of planning your business and keeping it running. The ideas and techniques in this chapter are just a start, you should be able to adapt to situations as they arise and plan for unexpected problems. With that in mind, now would be a good time to:

- ✓ Find a reliable locksmith. Tell them you are planning to start a vending machine business, and see what types of locks they suggest. Make sure that they can provide locks all keyed alike.
- ✓ Find companies that repair vending machines in your area. A good place to start looking for these is the vending machine distributors.
- ✓ If you already own machines, make sure that you have their manuals. If you do not, look on the manufacturer's website or call their customer support center.
- ✓ Find a vending machine repair course. Again, The Internet is an excellent place to start.

13

Record Keeping, Business Analysis, and Tax Planning

Necessary Office Equipment

The equipment in your office is as important as your equipment in the field. This equipment is used to keep track of your sales, product usage, inventory, contacts, suppliers, and finances. It is essential that it is in good working order and can be relied upon. The following is a list of items that will be needed in your office:

- Computer
- Fax Machine
- Telephone
- All-In-One Printer/Copier/Scanner
- Filing Cabinet
- Internet Connection

Most of these items will already be found in a modern home office and if not currently owned, can be purchased relatively inexpensively. As with most equipment, seriously consider buying used equipment as this will help keep costs low.

The computer will be used to purchase supplies over the internet, send email, and keep your records electronically. It is strongly advised that you do not buy the latest and greatest computer. Buying the most expensive computer you can find will only guarantee that you will have bought more than you need and wasted money. If you do not already own a computer or need an additional one, try buying a used system from one of the computer repair stores in your town. These stores frequently offer warranties that will protect your investment and ensure that you buy quality equipment. If you insist on new equipment watch for special from the large computer manufacturers and electronics retailers. Patience will be rewarded with significant savings.

The other items on the list above can be had very easily and inexpensively by checking out your local second hand thrift stores. You can usually find all of the remaining equipment in one of these types of stores and it should not cost you more than $100.

A Few Words About Record Keeping

Record keeping will be an extremely important activity that you need to conduct with diligence. Essentially, you need to keep a copy, if not the original, of every document your business receives of generates. You will need to have organized files that you keep orderly. Record keeping will be especially useful for:

- Budgeting
- Cost Analysis
- Tax Planning
- Profit and Performance Analysis

At the end of each month, take a few minutes and make sure that all of your new invoices have been filed along with all receipts. A few minutes periodically keeping your records tidy will save you hours of headaches searching for a lost receipt come tax time.

Tracking Invoices and Expenses

Tracking your invoices is another extremely important part of your office duties. If you do not keep track of your invoices, suppliers will not be paid promptly and you will lose vital information that can be used for tracking the health of your business.

The easiest way to track your invoices and receipts is to set them aside in a special location each month. When the month is over add up all of your invoices and receipts. There should be some form of documentation of every expense that you incurred over the month. If you have been diligent and each cost has been accounted for, this number will represent the total cost of operating your business over the course of that month. This number will be used for further business analysis.

You can also break the invoices and receipts down into specific categories to further analyze and track your expenses. Examples of these categories include but are not limited to:

- Food Items (candy, chips etc.)
- Beverage Items

- Machine Repair/Upkeep Services
- Vehicle Expenses
- Fuel
- Commissions
- Cleaning Supplies
- Machine Parts
- Rent
- Utilities (If applicable)

By breaking down these expenses you can determine increases or decreases in any of these areas. This will help you to decide which areas need to be given special attention to minimize costs and maximize your return on investment.

Once you have analyzed and paid your invoices, put each of them into appropriate files in your record system. Never under any circumstances throw away any invoices. You never know when they will be useful or needed. Lastly, remember that each invoice represents a possible tax savings come April 15th!

Tracking Income

The most important thing you do in the office is count up all the money that you take out of the machines. It is also probably the most fun part as well. However, there is a serious side to counting your piles of money that you need to remember. This is income to your business and is used to pay off any bills and to finance further business expansion if desired. This information, like any other that has so far been discussed needs to be recorded and analyzed to monitor the health of your enterprise.

When emptying a machine you will need to put the money from each machine into a separate bag. Separating the money in this manner will help you solve any money mysteries that should arise. When you get back to the office, count out each bag and record the total from each machine.

Once all the totals of all the bags have been recorded, you can compare these numbers to the route report that you filled out while servicing the machines. You will quickly be able to tell if every item has been accounted for in the money that you received. In the event that all products have not been accounted for, it could be due to double vending, misspends, or theft.

Over the course of the month keep track of all the income that you receive. At the end of the month total these numbers. This is your total income. You can also break this money down into smaller categories such as:

- Snack Income
- Beverage Income
- Frozen Food Income

ABC Vending Monthly Sales Analysis

Period: 8/1/06-8/31/06
Total Income: $10000

Item Category	Units Sold	Avg. Price	Income	Percent of Sales
Chips	2500	$.50	$1250.00	12.5%
12 Oz. Soda	3000	$1.00	$3000.00	30%
20 Oz. Soda	3600	$1.25	$4500.00	45%
Candy Bars	2500	$.50	$1250.00	12.5%

Total Units Sold	Total Income	Total Percent of Sales
11600	$10000.00	100.00%

Figure 13.1 This simple sales analysis shows that 20 ounce soda represents 45% of total sales and 12 ounce soda another 30%. From this information, ABC Vending can decide whether to continue to focus on soda sales or try to increase its snack sales

These numbers can help determine which categories are providing your enterprise with the most robust cash flow. Information like this can be useful in determining which types of machines need to be added to your business or locations that need more machines.

Profit Analysis

Once you have your total cost and your total income you can do some profit analysis. This is the famous "Bottom Line" and what any business boils down to.

Net profit is money that you have left over once all of your suppliers have been paid and your machine and inventory are back in the condition that you started with. This number is determined simply by:

Total Income – Total Cost = Net Profit

Your *return on investment* is the percentage by which you have increased the money you invested in the business.

For example, you invested $1000 in a vending business. Your total cost is $1000. Your income for one year is $1300. Once all suppliers have been paid, your net profit is $200. This represents a total increase in your investment by $200. You have replenished your inventory and repaired your machines to the same condition they were in at the beginning of the year, so you still have a business worth $1000 but you also have this pile of money worth $200. Your investment has increased by 20%, so your return on investment is 20% also.

The formula for return on investment is as follows:

100* (Net Profit / Total Cost) = Return On Investment

Another useful number to pay attention to is the percentage of total sales that is represented by a particular category of expense such as commissions or repair costs. Another example will be helpful.

Your total sales are $1000 for a given month. You pay out $150 in commissions that same month. You are effectively paying out 15% of your income in commissions. This is your commission cost. Remember, the goal is to have all of your costs, no matter what percentage of sales they represent, to add up to less than 100%. If they add up to more than 100% you are spending more than you are taking in. For a business that is undesirable.

The formula for category cost is:

100*(Category Cost / Total Sales) = Percent of Sales

Using these simple formulas you can keep close tabs on the health of your business. You will be able to see quickly if you are making the kinds of money that you would like to, and whether or not your costs are rising and falling.

ABC Vending Monthly Expense Analysis

Period: 8/1/06-8/31/06
Total Income: $10000

Cost Category	Amount Spent	Percent of Sales
Inventory	$4852.00	48.52%
Machine Repair	$450.00	4.5%
Commissions	$542.00	5.42%
Fuel	$527.00	5.27%
Vehicle Upkeep	$200.00	2%
Insurance	$525.00	5.25%
Rent	$500.00	5%

Total Income	Total Spent	Net Profit
$10000.00	$7596.00	$2404.00

Return on Investment

24.04%

Figure 13.2 This is a simplified example of a monthly expense sheet. Expenses are broken into categories and tracked as a percent of sales. Net profit and return on investment are also found through this sheet.

You should tabulate all of these figures at the end of each month and track them over the life of your business. These end of month reports should be compiled and set aside in a special file. You should also keep backup data somewhere secure. You should also compare your figures with the previous month's and year's (if available) each month.

Tax Advantages of a Vending Business

There are many potential tax advantages of owning and operating a vending machine business. If you are unfamiliar with the idea of itemized deductions and tax breaks a brief explanation follows. You can take advantage of these offerings to further invest in and grow your business.

Simply put, Uncle Sam has responsibilities too. The government would like to see jobs created and more tax revenue for the benefit of every citizen. To this end the Internal Revenue Service offers many breaks on taxes for business expenses.

Say for example you spent $1000 on business expenses the previous tax year and your income was $10000. The $1000 in qualified business expenses can be deducted from your business income. That means that you only are taxed on $9000 in income instead of the full $10000. If you are taxed at 15% you would only wind up owing $1350 instead of $1500. That is a difference of $150 that you can reinvest in the business that the government hopes will lead to more income (and more taxes) and more jobs at some point in the future.

The U.S. Tax code is a rather complicated set of rules and regulations that changes every year. Itemized deductions, such as the one described above, can be some of the most complicated parts of the tax code. In addition, if used improperly or without proper documentation, itemized deductions can mean costly mistakes in the event of an IRS audit. It is usually best to involve the skills of a qualified tax preparer when compiling business tax returns. Their expertise can save you many dollars and headaches and is well worth the cost of their fees.

However, there is no reason that you cannot start to plan to take advantage of these tax breaks before you ever walk into a tax office. With a little bit of knowledge you can plan to save yourself big bucks in taxes. The following three deductions are a great start. If you are interested in finding out every deduction you can (which would fill this book and many like it) a consultation with a tax professional is recommended. You can also learn many things from the IRS website as well (http://www.irs.gov).

Something else worth mentioning is that the following tax deductions refer specifically to federal income taxes. All 50 states have different and distinct tax codes and procedures. Some of these deductions may be applicable to your particular state tax system and others may not. This is definitely worth checking with a tax professional familiar with your state's particular system.

Business Miles

Operating a car is not free and with gas prices climbing ever higher, it is not cheap either. Businesses drive a lot of miles each year and this can represent significant costs in both fuel consumption and vehicle maintenance.

For tax year 2006, the IRS offers a qualified business deduction of 44.5 cents per business mile driven. That means for every one mile of business that you drive you can reduce your taxable income by 44.5 cents. That may not seem like a lot but consider if you are driving 10000 miles a year, you will reduce your taxable income by $4450. That represents a tax savings of almost $700 with the tax rate at 15%.

To qualify for this type of deduction and to have proper documentation in the event of a tax audit, you will need to have a mileage log. These are available in any office supply stores in booklet form. Many programs are also available for PDAs. You can always make one yourself with a spreadsheet or columnar pad.

Always remember to keep you mileage log updated and clear. Always keep copies as well. In the event of an audit or at the request of your tax preparer, you will need orderly documents.

Mileage Log

Company Name: ABC Vending
From: 1/3/06 to 1/10/06

		-Odometer-			-Fill Tank?-			
1	2	3	4	5	6	7	8	9

Date	Origin	Dest.	Start	End	Dist.	Y/N	Gal.	Desc.
1/3/06	Office	Loc. 1	45890	45895	5 mi.	No	0	Serv.

Total Miles:_____ Total Gallons:_____

I certify that the above information is true and correct to the best of my knowledge and that all mileage logged was for approved business purposes.

Signature:_____ Date:_____

<u>Figure 13.3</u> The above diagram is a simple and easy to use format for a mileage log. Column 3 records the destination. Columns 4 and 5 record the start and ending odometer readings. Column 9 record the very important purpose of the mileage.

Equipment Depreciation

Equipment acquisition is also a potential tax deduction. For each piece of equipment that you purchase for use exclusively with your business, the IRS will allow you to take 1/7 the value of the equipment as a deduction each year over the course of seven years. This is called equipment depreciation and can be used to defray the cost of buying equipment.

For example, you buy a new route van for $7000. Over the following seven tax years, you will be able to take a tax deduction of $1000 each year. At a 15% tax rate, this will save you $150 each year for seven years. At the end of the seven years you cannot depreciate the equipment anymore.

This type of tax deduction can be used for any type of business equipment from new vending machines to office computers, to route vehicles. To take advantage of this deduction you must have proper documentation, keep copies of any sale receipts and invoices for equipment purchases. If you buy equipment through private party sales, use an invoice book. These are commonly available in the business forms areas of office supply stores. Make sure to note the name, address and phone number of the other party involved. In addition get them to sign the invoice. Write down a description of the equipment that you are purchasing and the price. Give the other party the carbon copy for their records as well. When it comes to the IRS it is better to be overcautious with documentation now, then to be sorry later.

Inventory Deductions

Many people overlook this potential deduction. If you purchase inventory (soda and candy, etc.) during a particular tax year and have not sold the inventory at the end of that tax year, you can deduct the value of that inventory from your federal taxes. This can represent a large deduction if you stock up on supplies just before the end of the tax year. Either way, do a final annual inventory and make a copy for your tax file. You may be pleasantly surprised to see how much you can save. Your tax preparer will make use of this information to get you the deduction.

Conclusion

Maintaining efficient and organized records is an essential step to business success. Only by keeping these records and being able to access specific pieces quickly will you be able to analyze your business and take advantage of the tax benefits only hinted at in the preceding pages. To continue in the process of constructing your business plan you can:

- ✓ Purchase a filing cabinet. This will be helpful even as you organize your business plan and form your company. These

can be purchased in expensively from office liquidators around your area.
- ✓ Plan a mileage tracking system. You can either make your own using a spreadsheet program or purchase one at an office supply store.
- ✓ Learn more about accounting. This is a very good skill to have and is beyond the scope of this book. You can further your knowledge by, taking a class at a community college, or by reading books on the subject. Many public libraries have extensive sections on this subject.

14

Putting It All Together In a Business Plan

Once you have done all of the preliminary research and have decided on financing and business structure and have determined your entire permit and risk management needs, you will need to sit down and draw up a comprehensive business plan. If you have followed the suggestions at the end of each chapter, you already have a good foundation to build on.

Structure Of A Business Plan

The heart of a business plan is a strategy for the success of your business, put down on paper. Included in this strategy is a description of the business's activities, business structure, a marketing plan, necessary equipment, potential competition, potential customers and locations, lists of suppliers, insurance needs, permits, and descriptions of business operations.

In addition to information on the business and its operations, a business plan should include a thorough financial framework for your business. This part of the business plan should include, cost projections of the business, income projections, target income, break even analysis (the point at which you recoup your investment), and existing business cash flow analysis (this could stem from investments already held by the company or periodic cash investments).

Lastly, in the business plan, you should include any and all supporting documents that make executing your business plan easier. These documents should include tax returns (as far back as possible) of the primary investors, credit reports, resumes, corporate documents, IRS filings including Employer Identification Numbers, business licenses, permits, bank statements and lease agreements or proposals. All of these documents will be needed at some point during the formation and organization of your business so it will be of great benefit to have them all immediately available and organized.

Sample Business Plan

The following is a simplified example of a business plan for a vending machine company. This plan assumes that the company will be formed as an LLC.

Statement of Purpose

The purpose of this business plan is to outline the process and requirements of forming a vending machine company. Included in this business plan will be information on business structure, financial information, banking, permits and licensing, IRS filings, employees, marketing, machine placement, budgeting and risk management. Also included in this plan will be a checklist of pertinent documents to be used during formation.

I. Business Structure and Requirements

1. Business Description

The business that is being planned is a vending machine company. The primary business activity of this company will be the sale, through vending machines, of candy, soda, novelties and pharmaceuticals. The vending machines will be located anywhere a suitable customer base exists.

2. Company Formation

The company will be formed as an LLC. The name of the LLC will be ABC Vending LLC. At current there will be only one shareholder, but the possibility of future investors will be left open. The process of formation will be carried out by, Mr. Smith, a hired attorney. This formation will take place in the state of residence. According to the website of the secretary of state, the fee for the formation of an LLC is $400. This will be paid out of the primary personal account. The registered agent for the LLC will be the law firm of Mr. Smith. This process is expected to take between 4 and 6 weeks.

Once the Secretary of State has issued our UBI and Certificate of Formation, an application for and Employer Identification Number will be submitted to the IRS. This number will be required for all banking transactions.

3. Banking

Once the certificate of formation and the UBI for the LLC have been received, a business checking account will be opened at ABC Bank. This will be the primary checking account for ABC Vending. All operating expenses will be incurred by this account.

4. **Marketing**
Marketing in the vending industry is primarily directed towards obtaining new accounts. Product and location advertisement are not practiced as an industry standard.

The marketing for ABC Vending will be carried out through a collection of methods. These methods include but are not limited to:

- Cold Calling
- Flier Marketing
- Direct Mail
- On Machine Advertising
- Online Advertising
- Newspaper Advertising

In addition to the techniques described above, new locations will be added through existing account purchases.

5. **Suppliers**
Supplies will be obtained from several sources. For all classes of product (soda, snacks, novelty, and pharmaceutical) there will be a primary supplier and a secondary supplier. Most of these suppliers will deliver to a warehouse to be established in a mini storage park. Back up suppliers will not deliver

Soda will be obtained in both 12 oz. cans and 20 oz. bottles. An alternative supplier will be the local cash and carry supplier. Their prices are slightly higher, but if initial estimates of market demand are incorrect, or a rush on a particular product is observed, this supplier can serve to temporarily fill any shortfalls.

6. **Risk Management**
The areas of risk that need to be covered through insurance are product liability (risks associated with the products that will be sold through the vending machines), property and personal damage resulting from vending machines on location and risks associated with the business vehicles. A general liability policy can be tailored to fit these needs.

These needs will be discussed with Mr. Jones at ABC Insurance Agency.

7. **Permits**

A business license is required for all businesses that have sales above $25000 in our city. To start, ABC Vending may not be required to obtain a license, however, as a precautionary measure; our company will obtain a city business license. This license can be purchased from City Hall at a cost of $50.

In addition to a city business license, the city in which ABC Vending will operate requires vending machine licenses. These are issued for each machine and are purchased for $20 each. These will be purchased as the machines are placed on location and can again be purchased at City Hall.

8. **Personnel**

Initially ABC Vending will not need any additional staff beyond the owner. As ABC Vending grows this may change.

9. **Equipment**

ABC Vending will require the following equipment to begin operations:
- (4) 4-wide full size snack machines with bill validators $4000-$6000
- (1) Mini van with shelving for cargo $1500
- (1) Office computer $500
- (1) Set of Rol-A-Lift moving carts
- (1) Utility hand truck with moving straps $100

This is the minimum equipment needed before ABC Vending can begin operations. This equipment will all be purchased used. Soda machines will be provided through lease arrangements with the local soda bottlers.

9. **Operations**

The operations of ABC Vending will consist of finding new accounts and managing existing accounts.

New accounts will be obtained through the methods described in the marketing section.

Once accounts have been established, they will initially be serviced on a weekly basis. This rate can be increased or decreased as the needs of the accounts become more apparent. Machines will be filled using supplies obtained from the companies mentioned in the supplier section.

10. **Competition**

ABC Vending will be competing with a number of different types of operations. These types of companies are the local soda bottlers, large vending companies, and smaller independent operators.

Soda bottlers generally prefer larger accounts. These bottlers also do not provide snack machines. The business model of ABC Vending targets smaller locations that do want snack machines. This means that ABC Vending is not in direct competition with the local soda bottlers.

Larger vending companies are similar to the soda bottlers in that they prefer larger accounts. However, as these companies do provide snack machines, they can compete with ABC Vending for larger accounts. ABC Vending will deal with this problem by offering an extremely high level of customer service and professionalism to established accounts.

The largest source of competition will be smaller independent operators. These smaller vending machine companies prefer smaller accounts and can offer direct competition to all of ABC Vending's locations. Again, this competition will be met with high levels of customer service.

Contracts will not be used for any of the company's machine locations.

II. Financial Information

1. **Financing**

A loan application for a $10000.00 line of credit has been submitted and approved from XYZ Bank. This account will be used as a capital reserve to sustain ABC Vending through any unexpected costs and to take advantage of any sudden opportunities.

The rate on this loan is prime + 2%. This rate can be renegotiated in 12 months.

2. **Assets and Liabilities**

ABC Vending has $10000 dollar in cash on deposit in a high yield money market offering a competitive interest rate. This money should be used to purchase equipment. At this point all interest payments should be avoided unless absolutely necessary.

The only liability that ABC Vending has at this point is the annual agent fee charged by our law firm. In the event that the line of credit is used the monthly interest will become a liability. This should be avoided unless the prospective rate of return on the investment is greater than the interest rate on the account.

III. Document Checklist

- ✓ Corporate Operating Agreements
- ✓ Certificate of Formation with UBI
- ✓ EIN Certificate from IRS
- ✓ Tax returns of primary stockholders for the prior three years
- ✓ City business license
- ✓ Bank account numbers of existing accounts
- ✓ Copies of any proposed leases for rented property

Once you have written a plan like this and compiled all the relevant documents in a convenient folder, you are ready to begin forming your business and can do so in a well thought out, organized manner.

Conclusion

Once you have completed your business plan, print several copies and put them somewhere safe. You will need one for your records and others may wish to view it when opening bank accounts, applying for financing or when seeking insurance. They will also come in handy when meeting with your attorney or accountant.

<u>Afterword</u>

If you are reading this part of the book, there is a good chance that you have finished it. Hopefully, you found the information in it useful and informative and you now have a better idea of where to start in your quest to become a vending machine magnate.

No work is perfect from the start and any comments or suggestions for the improvement of this work will be greatly appreciated.

Before leaving you to get started, let me pass on a few words about integrity in business. You will be competing with other vendors but that does not mean that you cannot be friendly and helpful. Other vendors can be an invaluable resource for solving problems or finding things you need. If you consistently honor your word, conduct yourself professionally, and are helpful, you will often find others will often do the same.

That's it. It's up to you now. Good luck.

-Steven Woodbine

Vending Machine Fundamentals Vol. II

Success Strategies For Building Your Own Bulk Route

by Steven Woodbine

This book is dedicated to Paloma. Thank you for all your

In my first book, *Vending Machine Fundamentals: How To Build Your Own* Route, I focused most of the discussion on the subject of full service vending. That is, the business of placing soda and snack machines on location for the sale of refreshments. In that book, there was really little discussion of the business of bulk vending.

Since the publication of Vending Machine Fundamentals, I have received numerous enquiries from readers who wish for a more in depth discussion of the subject of bulk vending. This book is my answer to those enquiries.

In this book, you will find a detailed exploration of the business of bulk vending as well as how a small business enterprise can be constructed. We will start with a basic discussion of what constitutes a bulk vending operation and how it differs from the full service vending model. Additionally, we will discuss the many advantages of the bulk vending business to someone new to the vending industry. We will discuss how to build your business on a conservative budget and how to do so successfully. We will set goals specific to this type of vending and we will finish everything up with a business plan.

Throughout this work, I will refer to and incorporate pieces of information from my other book, *Vending Machine Fundamentals*. However, I want to assure you that this work will not simply be a reprinting of that book. Although I will reference this other book, there pieces will be identified as well as expanded with a much more focused approach to the bulk vending business model. Additionally, you will find a wealth of new information, again, specific to the business of bulk vending. This new information will focus on types of vending machines that were not included in the previous book as well as new product lines that were not explored in detail as well.

I also want to make clear that it is not necessary for you to have read my previous book to understand this one. This book will make clear the concept of bulk vending on its own.

When you are finished, I am confident that you will have the complete skill set necessary to start a bulk vending enterprise.

✓ Steven Woodbine

Chapter 1
Getting Started With Bulk Vending

Bulk Vending Defined

For the purposes of this book, we are going to define bulk vending as the sale of snacks and novelties through machines that require no electricity. These machines operate solely by mechanical means. Additionally, the machines that are to be discussed in this work only accept coins as opposed to full service machines that accept bills.

Many things can be sold through bulk and mechanical vending machines including, candy, nuts, gumballs, stickers, tattoos, condoms, non-prescription drugs, golf balls, diapers, tampons, jewelry, and toys.

This is a typical example of a bulk or mechanical vending machine. Coins are placed in the coin mechanism and loose product is dispensed. This particular unit is dispensing fish food.

It should be pointed out that there is another type of vending known in the trade as "full service" vending. This refers to the sale of merchandise through electronic machines with onboard computers and refrigeration units. This type of vending will not be discussed any further in this book. If this type of vending is of interest to you, please consult the first book in this series, *Vending Machine Fundamentals*. This title is available from the Pratzen Publishing website at www.pratzenpublishing.com or other online book retailers.

There are many types of mechanical coin mechanisms including these push in styles. This type is common on restroom vending machines.

History of Mechanical Vending

The first ever vending machine was a mechanical vending machine described by an engineer named Heron of Alexandria. Heron was a first century Greek inventor living in Roman Egypt. In one of his books, he described a machine that he had developed for vending water. A coin was dropped into a jug of water through a slot. The coin would then land on a pan. This would cause the pan to tilt down and open a valve at the bottom of the jug. Water would be dispensed for the washing of hands. When the angle of the pan was such that the coin slid off into the bottom of the jug; a counterweight would automatically close the valve and cease the dispensing of water.

Mechanical vendors as we know them today were only developed in the later part of the nineteenth century. The first mechanical vendors were used to sell gum, postcards and stamps. From there, these machines have been developed into the wide variety available today.

Why Bulk Vending?

Bulk vending is a business model that is commonly overlooked by the beginning vendor. People will often be drawn to the profit and growth potentials of full service vending. Machines will be bought and locations found, and that will be that. However, full service vending will often require much more investment, in terms of both money and time, to become a viable enterprise. Machines can cost as much as $2,000. In addition you will need to maintain large inventories with many product types to fill all of the selections available in the larger snack and soda machines. Lastly, the logistic of storing and moving machines of this size can become complicated very quickly.

None of this is true where bulk vending is concerned. I know a vendor who started with a single bulk candy machine. He had been given the machine as a gag gift a few years back, and one day on a whim, decided to see what would happen if they placed it on location. They made a few calls, found a location and drove the machine out in the back of their family car. They even filled the machine with candy they bought at a local supermarket. Done deal! That's how they got into vending. If you have to total up all of the costs for this scenario and even include the cost of a new machine you would be hard pressed to total the initial cost of starting this vending business at more that $200. I know a lot of people who will spend more that that going out to dinner in a week.

As the last example made clear, starting a bulk vending route can be a very inexpensive proposition. This is what makes it ideal for a beginning vendor. You can add machines as you need to and as your budget permits. Beyond that, you will not need to buy a new truck with a pneumatic lift gate to haul all of your equipment around. Most passenger cars will already work just fine for a beginning enterprise. Lastly, the amount of product that you have to keep in inventory to feed a bulk vending enterprise is small compared to full service vending.

The last quality that a bulk vending business has that makes it a good starting place for a new entrepreneur is that these types of vending businesses require much smaller time commitments than full service vending routes. Full service vending routes are commonly serviced once a week, usually operators will set aside an entire day to take care of their route. This is still better than a 9-5 job, but it is still a time commitment that needs to be maintained. On the other hand, bulk vending routes are commonly serviced on a monthly basis. It still may take a full day to service all of your machines, but it is already a quarter of the amount of time that you can plan on spending with a full service vending business. This makes it a great part time, income supplement that is perfect for working professionals, people with children, retirees and students.

Low Barriers To Entry

One of the greatest appeals of a bulk vending business are the relatively low barriers to entering the marketplace. When I first started with mechanical vending, all I invested was $50 for my fist machine and the cost of some products to sell. That was it! I added machines over time, built up my business, added product lines and eventually branched into the full service vending (the subject of my first book) as my main source of income. I know anyone can do it because I was 18 at the time and had only a minimum wage job to support me.

Additionally, there are always new locations to be had to the eager and self-motivated newcomer. New strip malls and businesses are always opening. Locations may grow dissatisfied with their current vendor this offers the opportunity for a new vendor to take over the spot. If you are dedicated and work hard, and conduct yourself professionally, you will find no shortage of locations.

When you compare these facts to the opening of a retail business, you quickly see how much easier it is to start a business of this kind. With a retail enterprise, you will need space, utilities, large and expensive inventories, complex licenses, and perhaps the most expensive cost of all; employees. These numbers can quickly run into the tens of thousands of dollars!

Benefits of Small Business Ownership

Anyone who has ever owned a small business can tell you that it can be a very rewarding experience. First and foremost, owning a small business can be a very profitable proposition. Beyond that, there can be financially beneficial tax advantages. This can include deductions to your income tax, as well as added benefits such as personal 401k plans, among others. For the most current and detailed list that is appropriate to your situation, you will need to consult a qualified tax preparer.

Beyond these advantages, a small business can allow you to create and grow an income based on how hard you work. This is not the case when you work for an hourly wage or a salary. However, always remember that when you work for yourself, the more money the business makes, the more money you as the owner make. This is a great motivator to many people.

Beyond simple financial advantages, there are other less tangible benefits. These include pride of ownership and the satisfaction of building a business that is solely yours. A lot of entrepreneurs will describe what they do with fondness and pride. It is something that needs to be experienced to be truly understood.

Profitability of Bulk Vending

Bulk vending has a tremendous profit potential when compared to soda and snack vending. With these types of products, there is commonly a 100% markup on each unit sold through the machines. This is a gross profit, but gives us a baseline with which to compare bulk vending.

Bulk vending products are often very inexpensive and are marked up by a large amount. This creates a tremendous profit potential for a vending machine investor. For example, 1 inch gumballs are usually sold in lots of 1000+. A recent price list from a reputable supplier listed a lot of 1500 of these gumballs for $52.00. If you divided $52 dollars by 1500 gumballs, you will arrive at a per unit cost of about $.035 or 3.5 cents. If you are selling these items for a quarter, you will arrive at a potential profit of over 700%! This is a great profit potential that should draw the interest of any investor looking to develop a small business income.

High levels of profit are not limited solely to candy sales, novelty items are frequently marked up to three or four times their cost. Condoms are sold in lots of 144 (also called "a gross") for about $30 per gross. Again, dividing the dollar cost of the lot by the amount of items in the lot, you will arrive at a cost of 20 cents per unit. Again, if you are selling these items for $1 per unit, you are looking at a profit potential of 500%.

Recent years have seen great volatility in the stock market. Market swings have wiped out large corporation and individual investors alike. Stability in this type of investing market can be hard to find. With this in mind, one can see why a few thousand dollars invested in a bulk vending business has appeal when you consider profit margins of several hundred percent.

How Much Will This Cost?

"How much is this going to cost?" is the question that any new entrepreneur should ask themselves. There is really nothing more important in the planning stages of a business venture than getting an accurate idea of the startup costs.

Fortunately, unlike many types of businesses, a bulk vending business CAN be a very inexpensive proposition that CAN be started without a lot of initial cost.

Bulk vending machines are not terribly expensive. In fact, in most cities around the country, you can buy basic, used machines in good condition for $50-$100 dollars. More elaborate machines can be more expensive, but the basic bulk vending machine model that you are familiar with will be in this price range. This means that you can add a machine to your route with product in it for around $100. Most of the time, the car you are already driving will be a sufficient vehicle for your new enterprise. This means that there is no cost for a vehicle. The only other real cost will be the formation of your business.

You Can Use An Organic Growth Model

In most cases, when you start a business such as a restaurant or store, you will need to make a large capital investment. You will need to rent a space, buy equipment, hire employees, and purchase inventory. These dollar figures can quickly add up and become daunting. It is true that to build a large vending business, you will need to invest money. However, a vending business is unique in that it is possible to add to it over time as success and your budget permit.

I like to refer to this as an organic growth model. You do not need to buy twenty machines to get started. Start with one machine, maybe a couple and add more when you find locations. Inventory can be added to keep pace with the number of machines that you have and you will be the only employee to start. This fact and the ability to grow your business organically is what makes a vending business so attractive to a new entrepreneur. This technique is one that you should definitely take advantage of when starting your enterprise. This keeps your risk low, provides you with an easier exit if you decide you do not like the vending business, and allows you to build up your experience and customer service skills before making larger commitments. This is also great training if you decide you wish to start dabbling in full service vending as well.

No Experience Necessary

It should be made very clear that it is not necessary to have any experience when getting started with bulk vending. Many of the operators I have known over the years started their successful businesses on a whim. They saw a cheap bulk machine and decided to buy it and give it a try. What is necessary is a good amount of common sense and problem solving skills. With these two abilities there is no real limit to where you can take your business.

Who Is Right For Bulk Vending?

I have been asked this question many times. The simple answer is that anyone who wishes to make a little extra money managing their own business is a perfect candidate for a bulk vending route.

More specifically a bulk vending route is right for you if you:

- Would like extra money
- Have free time during the business day
- Can commit 10-20 hours **per month** to this business
- Have extra money to invest
- Like working with people
- Are self motivated
- Are organized

People from any walk of life from a student, a stay at home parent, a working professional, or a retiree can fit this bill. I have known stay at home moms who serviced their route while their kids were in school. I set up my first location when I was a freshman in college and I have known vending route operators who were over 80! If you fit the criteria, there is no reason that a vending business might not be a good fit for you as well.

What Equipment Will I Need to Buy?

This is another great fact that makes a bulk vending business so easy to start. You really don't need to buy very other than your machines. One exception to this statement is a computer. In today's business environment, you need to be able to store records electronically as well as access the internet for the best pricing on supplies and machines. In the United States today, most people already have a personal computer. This will most likely do just fine. Remember, it does not need to be fancy.

A phone is the other type of business equipment that you will need to make sure you have. This can be a mobile or a landline. It does not matter. However, it will need to have voicemail. You need your accounts to be able to contact you as well as any customers or potential new accounts.

Phone Service For Your Small Business

When you start a new business, it is entirely reasonable that you do not want business calls coming into your personal or home phone. Many people will want to have a dedicated business phone, especially for the property stickers described in later chapters. Many new vendors will plan on receiving a large number of phone calls when they first start in business and will waste large amounts of money on business phone service. The truth is, that if everything is going according to plan with a bulk route, you will not receive many phone calls.

With the competition in the wireless phone service industry, there has never been a better time to seek out and find cheap business wireless service.

There are many options out there, and it will be up to you to decide which is the best fit for you and your budget. However, I will pass on several bits of advice. First, consider a prepaid phone. These are very inexpensive and can be purchased for as little as $10! Once you buy the phone, you will need to buy minutes on a prepaid card. These are a little more expensive by the minute, but the total overall amount of money that you will need to expend will be smaller than with any contracted monthly service.

You can also sign up for plans that come with a phone and a phone number, but no minutes. You will frequently need to pay somewhere in the neighborhood of $10 a month for this service as well. The only additional charge will be any minutes that you use. You will only be charged when you actually use the phone,

Both of these options are very inexpensive ways to provide your company with phone service if you decide it is necessary. Remember, there is no reason that it has to be necessary. You as the business owner must decide.

Business Service Stores

There is a good chance that your bulk vending business will be based out of your home or a storage locker. These locations are fine for carrying out operations, but they might not work for your administration needs. You might not be home when a package arrives, or you might not want your home address serving as the address of record for your business. Business service stores offer the solutions to these problems. A business service store is an evolution of the old copy machine store. These days, these stores offer many services.

Mail boxes are one of the main services offered by these stores. These boxes differ from post office boxes in that they are considered street addresses and can work for official business. Official correspondence such as bank statements, licensing, and business registration documents often need to go to a street address. Additionally, private carriers such as FedEx and UPS cannot deliver to post office boxes. After all, the Post Office and these carriers are in competition. This is again not the case with the boxes rented by business service stores. Private carriers can deliver to these boxes, and in fact, the staff of the business service store will be there to sign for any packages that come in.

Beyond mail boxes, these stores also offer other services that can be of use. One of the most convenient features to look for is fax services. Many of these stores offer dedicated fax lines which can, if a fax is sent to the attention of your box number, can receive faxes for your business. This additionally removes the need to have a dedicated fax line added for your business. These stores also can help with business card printing, shipping, and many other services that your new business will require.

What Kind Of Vehicle Do I Need?

Bulk vending machines, when compared to their full size counterparts are fairly small. In reality, you can easily start a bulk vending route with a basic sedan. You may need to put the seats down from time to time and make some extra trips, but you should be OK. Many families, use a mini van as their primary vehicle. These are an ideal vehicle to use on your route because they combine higher gas efficiency with a much larger cargo space. With one of these, especially if the seats are removed, you can easily carry all the candy you need along with extra machines and tools when you are servicing your route.

No matter what vehicle you own when you first start out a bulk vending business (that is as long as it is not a scooter or motorcycle), don't rush out and buy a new vehicle. Develop your business slowly with the resources that you have. As things progress and your business begins to earn you a reliable income, you may want to think about a vehicle upgrade, but not until that point.

A family mini van is more than enough to service a bulk vending route.

How Do I Form My Business?

How you ultimately decide to form your business is your decision alone. However, it is strongly recommended that you work with a licensed attorney before doing so. The professional advice and planning offered by a licensed attorney can be invaluable.

In Vending Machine Fundamentals, I discussed many different legal classifications under which you can form your company. However, in this work, for brevity I will only discuss the LLC corporate form.

An LLC, which stands for Limited Liability Corporation, is a recent addition to the world of corporate forms. Its creation arose from the desire of small businesses to obtain the added liability protection of a corporation, along with the simplified taxation of a sole proprietorship.

An LLC is formed by submitting Articles of Incorporation to the Secretary of State (this is generally accomplished through the state's corporations division). Articles of Incorporation are simply documents that spell out the rules of the corporation (such as entering and exiting), management of the corporation and such details as who is the agent of the corporation for correspondence, among many others. Stock documents, in which you only fill in the details, can be obtained from office supply and legal documents stores. However, it is recommended that these documents be prepared in conjunction with a licensed attorney who is familiar with the particulars of your state. Think of this as an investment in your company and be prepared to spend some money. Competent legal advice is always worth the cost.

Upon receipt of your documents, the Secretary of State will create your corporation. You will then be issued a Unique Business Identification Number or UBI, along with a certificate of formation. These pieces of information will be necessary to open bank accounts and conduct other affairs in the name of the corporation.

You may be asking yourself why all of this is necessary. There are several advantages to operating as a corporation. The main reason is the liability protection offered by a corporation. Essentially when you create a corporation, you are creating a separate legal entity from yourself. The corporation will have distinct tax identification numbers, bank accounts, and credit accounts from you as an individual person. Additionally, as a shareholder in the corporation, your liability may be limited to simply the amount of money you invest in the corporation. Anyone trying to sue you may have a great deal of difficulty in obtaining a judgment against your personal property. This is not always the case, and for the most correct and current information, your attorney is the best resource. However, this protection is something that should not be overlooked by a serious business person.

Other corporation forms (this includes S-Corps and C-Corps) have added taxation complications, including the possibility of double taxation and the need to file a separate tax return for the corporation. This is not the case with an LLC. Under current IRS rules, LLC are permitted a status known as "Pass Through Taxation". This is where income passes through the LLC untaxed into the hands of the shareholders (with a bulk vending route, this would most likely be a single person). Once the income is received by the shareholders, they simply declare the income on their personal tax returns, where the money is taxed. There is not double taxation or the need to compile a second tax return which can easily cost hundreds of dollars annually.

For these two reasons, an LLC is worth your time and money to form to protect your family and personal assets in the world of business.

How Do I Open A Company Bank Account?

Once you have formed an LLC, your business is going to need a bank. This is going to require you to go into a bank, present them with documents and make an initial deposit. To open an account for an LLC you will need to present the bank with your UBI number (this is on the certificate of formation from the state department of corporations) as well as an EIN.

An EIN is an Employer Identification Number issued by the IRS. This will be needed by your company even if you do not have employees and will serve a similar function to your Social Security Number in your personal financial matters. It used to be the case that you needed to file a form SS-4 with the IRS and wait for them to mail you your EIN. However, with the advent of the Internet, you now apply for and receive an EIN online in as little as 15 minutes. To do this, visit the IRS website at
http://www.irs.gov/businesses/small/article/0,,id=102767,00.html.

Once you have received the necessary numbers and documents, you will need to select a bank and make your initial deposit. The amount you will need to deposit can vary and may be as large as $1000. However, if you shop around, especially with local and regional banks, you may be able to find lower requirements. It is always a good idea to have a financial cushion, but business checking accounts rarely if ever pay interest, and you want to keep as little money in them as is truly necessary.

The last point that needs to be emphasized when searching for a business bank with a bulk vending business is the need of a favorable coin deposit policy. Remember, all the money you will be taking from machines will be in the form of coins!

Coin deposit policies can vary and may be as simple as the bank having a coin counter. Many standalone banks have coin counters, while bank inside of grocery stores will not. Some banks will take your coins in deposit bags to be credited to your account. These bags are then sent to a central counting facility. Once the money is counted, the funds will be deposited to your account. Either of these methods will work well for a bulk business. What you want to avoid is a bank that will only accept money in the form of rolls. This will necessitate you rolling all of the coins to be deposited. This can take a lot of your valuable time. If the bank you have selected will only accept rolled coins, continue your search for a bank.

Conclusion

In this short chapter, we explored many of the basic questions you should ask yourself before starting a bulk vending business. The truth is that a bulk or mechanical vending route can be started on almost any budget without any major capital investments. This added to the high profit margins and low barriers of entry make it a great business model for anyone seeking an pad their income.

Chapter 2
Bulk Vending Machines &Equipment

When most people think of bulk vending their mind automatically leaps to a simple gumball machine. However, in reality, bulk vending, for the purposes of this work, would best be described as "mechanical vending". In this book we will discuss many types of vending from gumballs, to stickers, capsules and even condoms, perfumes and diapers.

What we will not discuss is the business of full line vending, that is to say, soda and snack vending for large businesses. This has already addressed in the first book of this series, *Vending Machine Fundamentals: How To Build Your Own Route*. In this book we will only discuss bulk/mechanical vending.

Basic Bulk Vending Machines

The basic bulk vending machine will form the backbone of your mechanical vending route. They are simple to operate, gravity fed machines, with a single product hopper. When a coin is placed into the coin mechanism on the front of the machine, and the handle turned, gears inside of the machine rotate and permit to fall a preset amount of the product.

Basic bulk machines like this one will be common on your route.

These types of machines can be used to sell any kind of loose product from candy, to peanuts, to fish food! Additionally, many of the available models of machines of this type have variable price mechanisms that allow the owner to set the price from $.25 to $1.00. Coins fall from the mechanism into a collection point at the bottom of the machine.

These machines can be utilized on a table or countertop, but most often will be mounted on a metal stand about three feet tall. New, these machines will cost between $50 and $100. When buying machines of this type **DO NOT USE GLASS**! Glass is fine for a novelty machine on an executive desk but it is completely impractical for a machine in a commercial setting. One careless passerby can knock it over and cost you plenty of money in repair costs, not to mention an annoying mess. Instead, a professional vending operation should be outfitted with machines that use a composite (usually polycarbonate) product compartment. These materials are easy to clean, safe to store food in and will resist breaking quite a bit.

While these machines are simple to operate and inexpensive, they are limited in that they only sell one product. A possibly better investment of your money will be the next machine type we discuss, the multiple select bulk machine.

Multiple Select Bulk Machine

Basic bulk vending machines are perfectly good for a vending route, but are limited in one way. That is they only sell one type of product. If a customer does not like the single product that they offer, you will not be able to make a sale.

The multiple select bulk machine answers this problem by offering several different products. Two to four selections are common. If a customer is not interested in one, there is a greater likelihood that one of the others will be appealing and you can capture more revenue. You also cannot rule out multiple different product purchases by the same customer. This can more than double your revenue and profit.

These machines are essentially several different vending machines housed in a single case. There are separate product hoppers, and separate coin mechanisms that can all be set to a different price. Additionally, some models have separate coin boxes so you can determine which product is selling better. You can also tell this by seeing which product hopper has the least amount of product remaining in it when you service the machine.

This is a typical example of a multiple select bulk machine. Photo courtesy of OK Manufacturing www.okmfg.net.

These machines should form the bulk of the machines on a simple bulk vending route. Buy these over single machines any time you get the chance. The machines will cost about $150 brand new but can be purchased used as well. A fair price for a used machine would be between $75 and $100.

Spiral Gumball Machines

Spiral gumball machines are a little variation on a standard gumball machine. Instead of simply falling down a little chute and through a little metal door, these machines make a show of dispensing the product.

These machines stand about five feet tall with a globe at the top. The stand of the machine is about a foot in diameter and is a clear cylinder, with a spiral running down it. When the product is dispensed, the gumball rolls down the spiral and is dispensed a few inches from the floor. So, in return for the quarter, the customer receives a gumball and the thrill of watching it run down the spiral.

These machines offer a little more show than a standard bulk vending machine. The size and fun of the sale can help to increase revenue. It is also much harder to ignore the size of these machines. This helps to draw the attention of children and adults alike, making sales more likely. Think of a spiral machine purchase as an equipment and promotional investment in one.

This is a typical example of a spiral gumball machine. These tall colorful machines easily capture the attention of children and adults alike. This makes sales more likely. Photo courtesy of OK Manufacturing www.okmfg.net.

Spiral gumball machines cost a little more than a standard single or multi-compartment vending machine. New, these machines will cost about $500, depending on the manufacturer. Used these machines will cost somewhere between $150 and $200. However, the additional cost of these machines can be worth the cost. The added draw can increase sales. These machines are also more stylish than the basic bulk vending machines and this can be helpful in placing them on location. Lastly, the added size of the machines can make servicing less necessary. Some of these models can hold as much as 3000 1" gumballs!

Skill Vending Machines

Skill vending is a twist on the traditional method of bulk vending. These machines dispense spherical gumballs or superballs, however, instead of dropping down a product slot when the coin mechanism is engaged, the product drops into an area of the machine where the customer needs to remove the item through a second slot. This can involve a spring mechanism, like that on a pinball machine and shooting the ball through a goal. Some of these machines are actually foosball tables, in that the ball (actually candy) needs to be shot through a goal with two opposing players operating the little men. Either way, the ball will only become accessible to the customer, once they have satisfied the skill component. Foosball tables like the one shown below also increase sales. Think about it. Two people are required to play. This means that when one wins and chews the gum, the other will insist on one too.

This combined approach adds more value to the purchase in that they customer receives both a candy and some fun in skillfully retrieving it from the machine. Sports are popular with both boys and girls so there is a universal appeal. Also, many adults will be tempted to "play" these games as well by the addition of the skill component.

This is an example of a skill bulk vending machine. The ball or gumball is used as a ball in a foosball game. The winner gets the prize. Photo courtesy of OK Manufacturing www.okmfg.net.

These machines are a much newer addition to the world of mechanical vending and as such, are less common in the used market, however, they are not impossible to find. New these machines can retail for more than $1,200. If you have a location that has a high enough volume to justify the capital expense, like a mall or movie theater for example, these machines can definitely add to your bottom line and are worth considering.

Sticker Machines

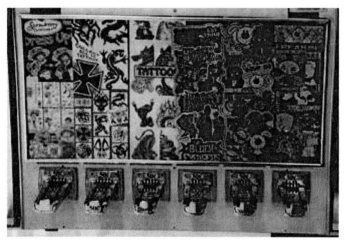

Sticker machines vend small, flat cardboard packages that are ideal for stickers, tattoos, and trading cards.

Sticker machines are a great addition to any bulk vending route. The colors and bight sparkles of stickers on display add a good deal of eye catching appeal to children. Also, the added product line will help to capture more revenue from each customer as, someone not satisfied with only candy, may spend those last few quarters on a sticker too. In some cases, this can double your revenue.

Another, related product line that can easily be sold through machines of this type is temporary tattoos. With tattoos being so prevalent in pop culture today, these items are in strong demand with kids. Do not overlook these when placing a sticker machine on location. In fact, make sure to devote at least half the selections of any machine to these.

The last popular type of product that is commonly sold in sticker machines is trading cards. These should be whatever is popular at the moment. Sports are a good staple, but don't limit yourself to just sports. Fantasy, celebrity and even political cards can be popular sellers.

Also, make sure that there is a good blend of stickers and tattoos in a machine that will appeal to as wide a segment of potential customers as possible. Do not load a machine with items that will appeal only to boys or girls exclusively.

Sticker machines will work well in a rack system, but can also do well on a single stand. Machines of this type vary in price depending on the number of available selections, but should not cost more than a few hundred dollars for a well built machine that will last a long time.

Capsule Vending Machines

Capsule machines like these, can be used to sell oddly shaped merchandise of all kinds.

Capsule vending machines are very common in rack systems and can frequently be seen in high volume locations like supermarkets, malls, and movie theaters. These machines dispense small round plastic capsules. The capsules themselves contain an item whose shape makes it difficult to sell through mechanical means otherwise.

All kinds of products can be dispensed through machines of this type. Small plastic toys, sticky devices, inexpensive jewelry, decorative arts such as woven bracelets, glow sticks, tattoos, erasers, dice and other items of this type are very common in capsule machines. Vending distributors will sell these items prepackaged for your convenience. You can also purchase empty capsules and package them yourself with whatever products you wish. This works very well if you get a great deal on a lot of stickers and do not have a sticker specific machine. You simply pack them in capsules yourself and load them into your capsule machines.

Capsule machines vend small plastic balls like this one. This permits items like jewelry and stickers to be sold.

Capsules machines come on two common sizes. These are 1" and 2" diameters. Always make sure your product comes packaged in the right sized capsule! You should always sell the right sized items in a machine. Mixing will only cause headaches. 2" capsules in a 1" machine will not vend, and 1" capsules in a 2" machine can cause multiple vends and even jams. Avoid the headache and use the machines as they were designed.

Capsule machines are not prohibitively expensive. New single machines will cost somewhere around $150 dollars, while used machines can be purchased frequently for $50-$100. Machines of this type can be mounted along with others to make a rack or alone on a stand. Either way, these machines can be good revenue generators and are worth your consideration for your route.

Rack Systems

It is common to place bulk vending machines that are on stands at locations. However, for high volume locations such as malls and grocery stores, a rack system is a better alternative, and by extension a more profitable one.

With a rack setup, you will not simply have just candy machines, but will have capsule and sticker machines as well. These machines do a great job of capturing revenue and will serve your company well if you have a location that justifies the cost of the equipment.

Rack setups offer a good potential for increased sales at high volume locations.

These machine banks are best placed at the exit point of a location if there are separate in and out doors. This is common in many grocery stores. The reason for emphasis on the exit door is to capture any coin change that has just been given to patrons. These large colorful machine combinations can draw the attention of children who will then ask their parents for change. With a little luck, the parents will turn over all of their coin change to the children, who will then in turn place every quarter they have into these machines until they run out. This can increase your total sales and greatly help the bottom line of your company.

The extra sales potential of these machines does come at an extra cost. These machine combinations can cost anywhere from $300-$1000, depending on the number of machines that are on the rack. Additionally, these combinations are large and heavy and will not fit in the trunk of a sedan. Instead, you will need a large van or even a moving truck to haul these machines around. This can cause an additional setup cost that needs to be accounted for in the decision to accept the location. However, if you have managed to secure a large location, and wish to make the investment, these machines can be very rewarding financially.

One last note, electronic, computer controlled, rack systems do exist. However, due to the complexity of these systems, they are expensive to purchase when compared to simple mechanical machines. Additionally, they require additional resources from the location. As such, these machines are better suited for a discussion on full service vending and are beyond the scope of this book. As such, they will note be discussed further.

Bathroom Vending Machines

Washrooms are an excellent place to carry out the operations in a mechanical vending business. There are many products that will sell, and sell well in bathrooms. Items like over-the-counter drugs, colognes, perfumes, deodorant, condoms of all types, panty liners, adult novelties, lip gloss, tampons, breath freshener, vitamins, and hangover remedies are all excellent inventory for bathroom vending machines.

Bathroom vending machines like this one can be a profitable addition to any bulk vending route.

Many of these products are oddly shaped and will not work well with the mechanical operations of a vending machine. To solve this problem, these products are sold inside small cardboard boxes like the one shown below. Like capsules, the packaging solves the problem of selling oddly shaped merchandise. These little boxes are stacked in a column with a weight on top. When the last item in the column is sold, a piece of metal on the weight will block the coin mechanism from working a prevent sales without a vend.

Bathroom vending machines dispense their products in small boxes. This allows items like cologne and condoms to be sold.

Bathroom vending machines are often described by the number of columns for different products that they possess. You will commonly encounter phrases such "four column machine" when speaking to machine suppliers. That being said, the price of bathroom vending machines varies by the number of columns that they have. However, used single column machines can be purchased for as little as $50. Some used condom machines can be had for even less than that!

Honor Box Vending

Honor boxes are one of the best kept secrets in the vending industry. As the picture below shows, an honor box is nothing more than a specially shaped cardboard box that also has a cardboard money box. What makes an honor box different from other types of vending machines is that it is not a machine. There is no lock and no mechanism and nothing to keep someone from simply taking all of the snacks, other than their honor. That's where the name comes from.

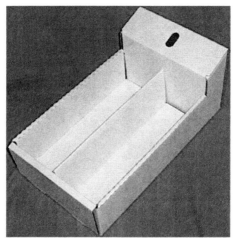

Honor boxes make a great addition to a bulk vending route. Photo by Bridget Cribben provided courtesy of Cameron Packaging. For more info on Cameron Packaging's honor boxes visit
http://www.cameronpackaging.com/snackboxes.html

The products that are sold through honor boxes are not the same types of snacks that are sold through bulk vending machines. Instead, they are the same types of snacks that are sold through full service snack vending machines. However, instead of machines costing hundreds if not thousands of dollars a piece, these boxes cost less than $3 each. Completely loaded with products, the total cost of placing an honor box is less $50 depending on the type of snacks that are placed in the box.

At this point, you might be wondering who in their right mind would be willing to build a vending business based on people's honesty. The fact is that honor box vending is a highly successful type of vending. You may be surprised a great deal when you check the coin box and find that is full of your money, sitting safely and undisturbed. If you couple an honor box vending business with charity sponsorship, like that which will be discussed later, you will find that incidences of theft drop very low. Many people will find it completely unimaginable to steal from the helpless and needy.
Lastly, even if there is theft of the entire box and all the snacks that it contains, how much money will you have lost? Compared to the cost of losing a full sized vending machine and its entire contents (this has happened to me more than once) the costs are almost not even worth mentioning.
There are many other advantages to honor box vending, beyond their low startup cost. Honor boxes are easy to transport. They will fit in any vehicle out there and can even be carried on foot if needed. Buying honor boxes is simple as well. They are collapsible and easily shipped in the mail. This makes it possible to shop around and find the best price as well as receiving them quickly.

Honor boxes also take up a very small amount of space. Depending on the particular configuration of your box, they will require less than two square feet of counter space. This makes them ideal for a location that are promising enough for you to sell snack foods at, but that does not have room for a full service vending machine. Additionally, the fact that honor boxes do not need electricity means that they can be placed anywhere. The lack of any cost to a location as well is a big plus when selling a manager on your services as a vendor.

One last benefit offered by honor boxes is to the bottom line of your vending operation. Bulk vending machines are great and can be very profitable. However, gross profits from a bulk vending machine sale are between $.20 and $.40. However in an honor box, you can sell more expensive snacks with profit margins as high as $1.00 without having to take on all the additional complications associated with full service vending. That is why this subject is included in this book on bulk vending and why you should definitely consider offering this service on your route. You really have very little to lose and a lot to gain.

You can also treat honor boxes as an additional added service later in the life cycle of a vending location. Perhaps start a location out with a simple bulk machine. Then if sales are good, consider offering them an honor box to increase your sales and diversify the offered product line. You have very little to lose and only more money to gain. Additionally, honor boxes can be offered to many small and medium sized businesses that already have full service soda machines. Many vendors will not want to "waste" a snack machine on a small time location. You can pick up the money that they are leaving behind. This can also open the door to establishing a bottler serviced full size route later on, like the kind discussed in the first volume of this series, *Vending Machine Fundamental: How To Build Your Own Route*.

Honor box vending is not without its downsides as well. You will experience thefts from time to time. However, this is true in every type of vending operation. You should come to grips with that before you ever place your first machine. Additionally, there will be more types of products for you to manage in your inventory. While this is not a horrible burden, it is one more thing for a new vendor to keep track of. However, with all that in mind, you should definitely give this type of vending some serious consideration.

Mint Boxes

Mint boxes are a cross between basic bulk vending machines and honor boxes. Like the basic bulk vending machine, these displays have a gravity fed hoper that is filled with some type of candy. It is best if the candy is wrapped or packaged. Peppermint patties that are wrapped in foil are very common and give this type of vending its name, however many different types of packaged candy will work just as well.

Like the honor box, these displays make no effort to safeguard the contents. If people want to steal from them, most of the time they will be able to. However, again, like the honor box, these displays are commonly left completely unharmed and when a piece of candy is taken, it is almost always paid for. One of the way to ensure this, even if the mint boxes are displayed to the public, is to, again, partner with one of the charity vending programs that are discussed shortly. This can very easily all but eliminate any theft. You might be surprised how well these little boxes can sell!

These displays are made of rugged acrylic plastic and can stand up to lots of abuse. They are also easy to clean. Also, as they are small they are ideal for locations that do not have a lot of space to spare but are willing allow a placement. New, these displays commonly cost between $25 and $50 dollars depending on the size and color of the plastic.

Locks

Locks are a very important part of your equipment as a bulk vending operator. After all, without locks, you won't make any money. The basic lock type that will be used on mechanical and bulk vending machines is a cam lock. A cam lock (pictured below) is a simple brass or steel lock that turns an arm when the key is turned. This arm in turns prevents the panel from being removed. The two common compartments that are locked are the product compartment and the cash box. It is not uncommon for both compartments to have separate locks.

This is a typical example of the cam locks employed on bulk and mechanical vending machines.

Cam locks tend to be lower security locks. This means that you need to be very cautious as to where your machines are placed. Never put a bulk vending machine outside. The brass that some locks are made from can be easily drilled out in less than a minute. I have even known machine locks to be broken with nothing more than an Allen wrench!

If at all possible, have all of your machines keyed in a similar manner. You can buy matching locks and install them as necessary. A locksmith can help with this. It is not a bad idea to have one key for the product compartment, and one key for the cash boxes.

Conclusion

All of the machines that you will need to build a bulk vending business have been described in this chapter. It would not be a bad idea in the planning of your business to begin searching your area for machine suppliers. You can also look on the internet as well. Start thinking about what machines you would need to purchase, and begin to price them, new and used. This will help with budgeting so, when the time comes to start buying machines, you will be well prepared.

Chapter 3
Bulk Vending Products

Not All Products Are Appropriate

When you first start out in vending, you will often want to sell anything and make as much money as you can. That's great! I wish you all the luck in building a little vending empire. However, some products should be avoided when you are first starting out. Chief among the list of things to avoid are stamps and prepaid calling cards. There is no profit margin in stamps. They are really only sold as a customer convenience, not a profit generator.

Prepaid calling cards can be profitable. However, they can also be a problem. You need to be certain that the company whose cards you stock is reliable. After all, your young company's reputation is on the line. In recent years, there have been a number of frauds involving prepaid calling cards. Additionally, these cards expire and if they are not sold within an allotted time, they can become worthless.

Newspapers are another product that are sold through automatic machines as well. These are also to be avoided by a bulk vending operator. These should be owned by the newspaper companies.

Bulk Candy

Bulk candy will be the bread and butter of any successful bulk/mechanical vending enterprise. These machines are very common and are found in any type of business in America today. There are many, many different types of loose candies that can be sold through machines of this type. In fact, there are so many, they will not all be listed here. Instead, a broad overview of the candies that can be sold through your machines will be presented.

Bulk candy like these jelly beans will be the mainstay of any successful bulk vending route.

Chocolate Candies

Many of the candies that you will stock in your machines are going to contain chocolate. This can include solid candies, as well as candies that have chocolate shells like M&M's™ or Reese's Pieces™, or chocolate covered candies like malt balls, espresso beans, or peanuts.

Chocolate products are a great draw, and if you are operating multi-head machines, should always be represented in the available selection. The one thing that you need to be aware of with chocolate candies is that they can melt. This can present a problem in summer months and will ruin any candies that do melt. Additionally, a hopper full of melted candy is a real mess to clean up. If any candies are found to have melted, you will need to remove and dispose of them, as well as clean and inspect the machines to make sure it is still serviceable. It is best to stock these candies only in climate controlled environments.

Fruit Candies

Fruit candies are probably the best type of candy to sell through bulk vending machines. Mike & Ike's™, Skittles™, and Runts™ are always good sellers in bulk machines. These candies are inexpensive in bulk packages, have wide appeal and stand up fairly well to higher temperatures. Additionally, the very colorful nature of these products can add eye catching appeal to a machine. These product lines may be shaped like fruit, or just flavored with fruit, but are always popular sellers. This type of candy should almost always be represented at any bulk vending location that you operate, even if it is the only item that you sell.

Sour Candies

Sour candies are a subset of candy. Many different candies can be made sour. In fact, there are many, many candies that can be called sour. These products include, but are not limited to, Lemonheads™, Sour Skittles™, SweeTARTS™, Warheads™, and Cry Baby™. These candies are durable and do well in bulk machines. Sour candies tend to be a little more expensive than other candies, but they also tend to be strong sellers. Additionally, these candies are almost all very colorful which adds eye appeal to your machines.

Jelly Beans

Jelly beans are a great classic candy to be sold through bulk vending machines. They are easily recognizable, hold up well to higher temperatures, come in a wide variety of flavors and are a popular candy to begin with. Additionally, the colorful nature of jellybeans can be a great eye catcher. In recent years, specific brand names of jelly begins have begun to introduce unique flavors that are appealing due to their unappealing nature. This can include flavors such as vomit and fish. People find these very fun and this can be an added draw to sell more product. No matter what type of jelly beans you choose to stock, they are always a good staple choice.

Wrapped Candies

Wrapped candies can be sold through bulk machines provided that their dimensions will work with the mechanics of the machine. This increases the type of products you can carry by a large factor. If you are ever uncertain that a product will work with your machines, by all means investigate and test it out. If it jams the machine, of course it will not work. If on the other hand, it works, you have a new product line.

Even if a particular candy does not work with you machines, this does not mean that it does not have a home on a bulk vending route.

Remember when we talked about honor boxes and mint boxes in Chapter 2? These candies work perfectly with these sales outlets.

Sugar Free Candies

Diabetes is on the rise in American as is obesity and health consciousness. This has created a market demand for candies that are sugar free. This market demand has been answered with sugar free versions of many of the most popular candies in production. This list includes sugar free jelly beans, hard candies, jawbreakers, wrapped products, mints and fruit candies. Prices range on these candies and they do tend to be a little more expensive than the sugared varieties, but they may be worth exploring for your route. They may add healthy amounts to your bottom line.

Cinnamon Candies

Cinnamon candies are very popular and are enjoyed by many people who enjoy the spiciness that they offer. One only has to look to the Hot Tamales™ product to know that these candies are sought after and are good sellers in any bulk vending machines. Red Hots™ are another very popular type of cinnamon spicy candy. These are small (less than 5 mm) candies that are chewable. They pack a pronounced cinnamon punch. Because of their small size, these candies are also easily sold through most bulk machines.

The last type of candy that will be mentioned in this section is the cinnamon "fireball". These are large chewable candies that are very spicy. These candies are eaten whole and cause quite a flavor sensation. These candies are similar in size to gumballs with an overall diameter of about one inch and work well in bulk machines

Gumballs

It might seem odd to think that the subject of gumballs would require any exploration, but this is the case. Gumballs are one of the original and best selling items to be sold through bulk vending machines, and certainly, these candies will have a place on your route. As, we have already discussed, there are even giant novelty machines specially designed to sell lots of gumballs.

Gumballs come in many different sizes ranging from half an inch to 1.25 inches in size. The most commonly encountered size both from suppliers and in the field are the 1 inch ball. This is the candy that many of the novelty machines are designed to sell.

Additionally, instead of simply being bland flavored gum as was the case in the past, there are now many different flavors of gumballs including, but not limited to:

- ✓ Cherry
- ✓ Cinnamon
- ✓ Blueberry
- ✓ Sour Apple
- ✓ Peach

Also, gumballs are produced that have patterns on the surface. For instance, gumballs are made that look like baseballs, soccer balls and even human eyes! These can add appeal depending on the time of year (Halloween) and can help boost sales as well. The best course of action when stocking a gumball machine is to fill it with an assortment. This maximizes the appeal of the products in the machine (which are visible) and increases the possibility of vends.

Gumballs are also a very inexpensive product line to carry. Basic gumballs frequently cost less than $.03 when purchased in bulk. Designer balls, like those made to look like eyes, will cost about $.05 per unit. If you sell these items for $.25, your company can realize a gross profit range of 80%-88%.

Jawbreakers

Jawbreakers are large spherical hard candies that are great sellers in bulk machines. These candies are offered in many different flavors, and many distinct patterns just like gumballs. You will be able to find marbled patterns, and even eyes and baseballs. Additionally, jawbreakers come in many different sizes and can be as large as 4 four inches in diameter. Prices of around $3 per pound are common. These candies can be sold through normal bulk machines or the spiral machines that were described in Chapter 2.

Peanuts

Peanuts are always a popular item to sell through bulk vending machines. These salty snacks are especially welcome in bars where they make people thirsty and encourage the sale of additional beverages. I have known bars that had a bulk vending machine on every table. Think about one of your machines on every table in a bar packed full of people. This is never a bad pitch to a bar owner.

There are three commonly sold types of peanuts that you should be familiar with. The first is dry roasted, salted peanuts. These are the basic peanuts that people think of when they hear the word. These are easily sold through bulk machines. Additionally, there are honey roasted peanuts that combine a sweet and salty flavor that is appealing to many people. The last type of peanut variety that you might think about selling is peanuts in the shell. These peanuts need to be extracted from the shell and give people something to do with their hands. Peanuts in the shell do have one downside that you should be aware of. This is the fact that the shells have to go somewhere. You cannot trust customers to dispose of them properly. This means that they will wind up on the floor as a mess to be cleaned up. This makes peanuts in the shell harder to sell to a business owner.

There is one big concern when you choose to sell peanuts through bulk machines. This is the fact that some people are deathly (literally) allergic to peanuts. People with this allergy can react to even the smallest amount of peanut residue. This means that once a machine has been used to sell peanuts, it cannot be used to sell any other type of product. Consult an attorney for more detailed and the most current and relevant information on peanut product liability and warning labels.

Condoms

Condoms are a great product line to add to any bathroom vending operation. This becomes especially true in bar and nightclub environments or any other place that adults gather. These products also offer a valuable community service in that they help to prevent the spread of the HIV virus along with other sexually transmitted diseases.

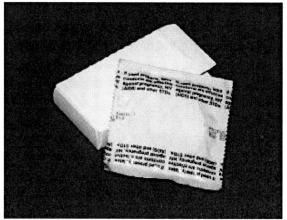

Condoms are a great item to sell in bars, colleges, nightclubs, etc.

Condoms, like most bathroom vending products are sold in small cardboard packages. There are many different brand names that can be sold; as well as different types of condoms. These include, but are not limited to:

- **Lubricated** – These condoms are pre-lubricated.
- **Spermicidally lubricated** – These condoms are lubricated with a spermicidal jelly (usually nonoxyl-9) for added birth control properties.
- **Studded** – These condoms have raised studs along the length of the condom for heightened sensation during intercourse.
- **Ribbed** – These condoms have raised ridges that run the length of the condom. Like studs, the purpose of these ridges are for enhanced sensation during the sexual act.
- **Flavored** – These condoms are flavored with an edible, sweet flavored lubricant. Flavors commonly include fruit flavors like cherry, peach or even pina coloda.
- **Ultra thin** – Ultra thin condoms are often sold as heightened sensation condoms. These condoms have thinner walls and are supposed to increase sensation during sex.
- **Colored** – Colored condoms have a novelty appeal that helps to sell them. On these condoms the latex is colored with vibrant hues.

- **Glow in the dark** – Like colored condoms, glow in the dark condoms have a novelty appeal that can make them popular sellers. These condoms do actually glow in the dark.

Most varieties of condoms are sold by the gross (144 units) and cost around $.25 per unit. These products can easily be sold at retail prices of $.75-$1.00 per unit, or a 200% mark up. Condoms do have an expiration date that you will need to take into account in your inventory management.

Perfumes & Colognes

Perfumes and colognes are a commonly overlooked product line to sell in bathroom mechanical vending machines. These products are sold in small cardboard boxes like the one shown below.

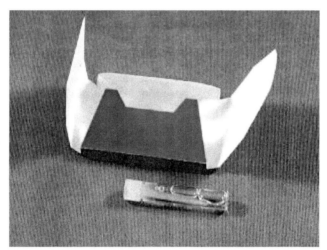

Perfume is often sold in glass vials inside cardboard packaging.

Inside the small box, you will find a small glass vial of perfume or cologne. These are best sold in bathrooms as a convenience. A man or woman who suddenly discovers the unwelcome presence of body odor can address it in a quick, cost effective manner.

Hangover Prevention/Treatment

In recent years many products have begun to be marketed as "hangover remedies". These products should be considered a nutritional supplement and not as a medication. In fact, medical science has not proven that these products work. However, they can be popular sellers in a bar environment, and as such, they will be mentioned here. Most of these "remedies" are just a dose of essential vitamins. Many of these vitamins are depleted during a night of drinking and the supplement simply helps to replace these. If you are interested in selling these products through your machines, start with a vending distributor. These specialty businesses will be able to offer you the most current line of products as well as pricing.

Toys

Toys are a fairly large and generalized category of items that can be sold through bulk vending machines. This category can include balls, whistles, sticky hands, plastic figurines, key chains, flashlights and many other amusing novelties that kids find appealing. Due to the odd shapes of items in this category, toys are almost always sold through capsule vending machines.

Toys are a great series of items to sell through capsule machines.

For the latest types of toys that are sold through capsule machines, consult the catalog of a bulk vending supplier. They will be able to provide the most current list.

Toys do tend to be a little more expensive than many of the other product lines discussed in this chapter. This is partly due to what they are made from. Unlike thin latex for condoms, or paper in the case of stickers, many toys employ larger amounts of plastic and even metal in their construction. This raises the cost. A fairly common range of cost associated with toys would be $.25-$.40 per unit at wholesale.

Temporary Tattoos

Tattoos have gone from being taboo to being chic. Accompanying this dramatic rise in popularity, temporary tattoos have also increased popularity. The tattoos themselves are sold in small cardboard boxes or sleeves and can be applied using water. Temporary tattoos can also be sold through capsule packaging.

After a few days these tattoos wear off but during those few days, the tattoos are shown off with pride. Young people want to appear distinct and younger kids want to show the same tattoos as celebrity idols and their older siblings. The business of temporary tattoos has even been harnessed by the advertising industry in recent years as a way to get people to proudly display company logos on their bodies for a few days free of charge.

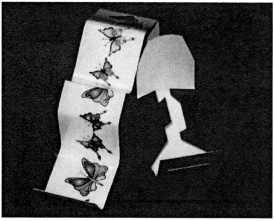

Temporary tattoos like the kind shown in this picture can add healthy sales to your company's bottom line.

There are many different types of tattoos that you can stock you machines with. Tribal tattoos are simple black patterns. There are also cartoon characters, religious tattoos (showing of a particular religions symbols or phrases), comic book heroes, sports tattoos, specifically branded girl tattoos. Costs on tattoos vary depending on the packaging and the design of the tattoo, but a fair price range is about $.10-$.28 per unit. With a retail price of $.25-$1.00, these units can be a very profitable product line to carry in your machines.

Stickers

Stickers are sold through the same mechanisms as tattoos. These are capsules, small cardboard boxes and cardboard sleeves. Many of the same designs that are available for tattoos are also available in the form of stickers. Again, the list includes tribal patterns, super heroes, cartoons, sports logos, etc. Essentially, one could even think of stickers and tattoos as the same patterns simply adhered in different manners. There are also stickers associated with popular music groups as well as movies and television shows. If you choose to buy these, you need to be aware and relatively certain of the fads continuing popularity. Otherwise, you could find yourself with an inventory of stickers that cannot be sold because the movie or music group are no
longer popular.

Stickers are commonly sold through cardboard sleeves like these, as well as in capsules.

Stickers are commonly sold in units of one gross (144 pieces) at prices per unit of between $.10-$.25 per unit. These units can easily be sold at retail prices of $.50-$1.00. Displays for your machines (to help sell them) are often included when you purchase stickers.

Jewelry

Jewelry is a great product line to offer through capsule machines. There are many different types of jewelry that can be offered including pieces made from metal, plastic, acrylic, and braided thread. It is common to think that this type of product line will appeal to girls only, but this is a misconception and one should not underestimate the appeal that shiny objects have over both genders. Most product lines available will have a designed unisex appeal.

There will be three basic types of jewelry that you can sell through your machines. These will be necklaces, rings and bracelets. These products will be sold in bulk units of 100-250 with a cost range of $.10-$.20. With a target vend price of $.50-$1.00, these items can be very profitable and will often work well in conjunction with other capsule lines. These items almost always come prepackaged in capsules. Like other capsule machine product lines, you will also receive printed, professional looking material to place in the front of your machine to help sell these products.

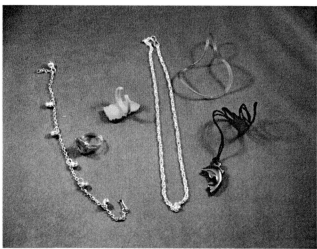

Jewelry sold through capsule machines can easily add to your bottom line.

Diapers, Tampons & Sanitary Napkins

Diapers and sanitary napkins tend to be avoided by vendors and often fall more into the realm of a custodial convenience. That being said, there is no reason that they should be excluded from this work, or your route necessarily. They are simply another product line to consider and analyze for profit potential. If the opportunity to sell these items profitably arises, there is no reason that you cannot seize it. Remember, a vending route is your business and you always decide what is best.

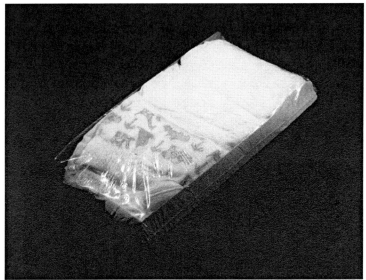

Packaged individual diapers, like this one can be sold as a convenience through mechanical bathroom vendors.

The best place to locate machines that sell these items is of course in public bathrooms. This will expose machines to the largest amount of customers. Of course, tampons and sanitary napkins are appropriate for women's rooms only. Diapers can be sold in either gender's bathroom.

OTC Drugs

Over the counter drugs can be a great source of revenue for your business. Unlike candy or other consumables, these products are not impulse buys. Ask anyone with diarrhea if pills that can make it stop are a necessity. Additionally, these medications have a great profit margin. Many of the medications can be purchased for $.25-.$.60 per unit and can easily be sold for $1.00. The best locations for machines selling OTC medications are generally in bathrooms, in machines that can also be used to sell condoms and perfumes.

Many of the medications that will be discussed will be available in generic form, as well as name brands. It will be up to you as a business owner to decide which product you wish to sell. Generic brands are cheaper and can often generate a higher profit, however, name brand packages have a way of selling themselves.

Painkillers

Painkillers are probably the most sought after over the counter medications. They are used to treat headaches, toothaches, back pain, sprains, bruises, migraines and a host of other minor ailments. These types of pills are also great for treating hangovers. These pills should be in any lineup of OTC medications.

There are four common medications that are used as painkillers. You should know them by the chemical name as well as the common trade names that these medications are sold under.

Four commonly sold painkilling medications are:
- **Acetaminophen** This medication is a common treatment for fevers as well as headaches. This medication is commonly sold under the Tylenol™ label.
- **Ibuprofen** Ibuprofen is a commonly used Non-Steroidal Anti-Inflammatory (NSAD) drug commonly sold under the trade name Advil™ or Motrin™. This medication is used to reduce swelling as well as treating minor pain.
- **Aspirin** Aspirin was the first NSAID drug to be manufactured. This drug is commonly sold under the Bayer™ trademark. This medication, like ibuprofen, is used to treat minor aches and pains.
- **Naproxen Sodium** Naproxen Sodium was first sold in 1976 as a prescription. Currently, this medication is available in the United States as an OTC painkiller, sold under the trade name Aleve™.

Anti-Diarrhea

Anti-diarrhea medications are another great source of revenue that can be sold through your machines. After all, when someone wants one of these medications, they really need one. These medications are used to stop cramping, diarrhea, vomiting, nausea and other problems with the digestive system. Two common medications are used to treat these problems. The first of these is bismuth subsalicylate, commonly sold as Pepto-Bismol™ and the second is loperamide, commonly sold under the name Immodium™.

Antihistamines

Antihistamines are a class of drugs that fight histamines in the body. Histamines are responsible for inflammation and allergies including stuffy nose, itchy and watery eyes, as well as hives and rashes.

The most common commercially available antihistamine, for vending, is Benadryl™. This particular medication tends to be more expensive than many of the other medication that are discussed in this section. Packages of these pills commonly cost about $.40 per unit. These packs include two pills.

Decongestants & Cold Remedies

It is not uncommon to confuse antihistamines and cold remedies. Both deal with clogged noses and sneezing. However, in reality these medications treat different underlying conditions with different medications. These mixes usually include a painkiller, frequently ibuprofen to help break fevers, as well as a nasal decongestant. The nasal decongestant is usually psuedephedrine or phenylephrine. You should be aware that the sale of psuedoepherdrine is controlled in many areas due to its role in the manufacture of methamphetamine. If this chemical is controlled in your area, DO NOT STOCK IT. If it can be sold at all, there are tracking procedures that you will not be able to comply with using automatic machines. If you sell this product without complying with these regulations, you will be in violation of the law and could be subject to fines and prosecution. Skip the headache and consider stocking products with phenylephrine. Most drug manufacturers that manufacture cold remedies make versions with either chemical for this very reason.

Pricing for these mixes are comparable to other OTC drugs and should cost between $.25-$.30 per unit with retail prices of $.75-$1.00 or higher.

Antacids

An antacid is a medication that is used to control the acids in the stomach and accompanying symptoms which include indigestion and heartburn. The main ingredient in an antacid mixture is usually a chemical known as a base. In most commercially prepared mixtures, this chemical is calcium carbonate. This chemical mixes with and neutralizes stomach acids. Common brand name antacids are Tums™ and Rolaids™.

The main ingredient in these pills, calcium carbonate, is very inexpensive. This means that the pills made from it are also inexpensive. It is not at all uncommon to find individual packages of antacids costing less than $.10 in wholesale lots.

Cough Drops/Sore Throat Relief

Anyone who has ever had a really bad sore throat or cough knows how unbearable they can be. This is what makes these types of medications or remedies such a popular line to keep in your machines. This becomes ever more true during the fall or winter months when colds are on the rise. Let's be honest, at this point these items sell themselves.

Most of these types of medications have a per unit cost of under $.25 with a potential vend price of between $.75 and $1.00.

Dramamine

Dramamine is a medication that is used to treat the vomiting and nausea that is associated with air sickness, car sickness and sea sickness. This medication is commonly sold in airports, marinas and highway rest stops. If you have a bathroom machine that is located in an area that would encounter people fitting this description, Dramamine might be a good medication to stock. Locations that might be appropriate are hotels and restaurants right off the highway, or a business next to a river or lake where boaters frequent.

Stimulants

When discussing stimulants in connection with over the counter medications, the only chemical that is commonly used is caffeine. Two commonly available formulas are No-Doz™ and Vivarin™. The pills are used as alertness aids and offer caffeine equal to amounts found in several cups of coffee.

Caffeine pills are lower in cost than many of the other medications discussed in this chapter. Common pricing for individually packaged caffeine pills is around $.20. Retail pricing can be up to $1.00 or even higher.

Anti-Cramping Medications

Anti-cramping medications are pills that are specially formulated to deal with the symptoms of menstruation. The treated symptoms include cramping, bloating and water retention. These medications are usually a combination pain reliever such as acetaminophen as well as a diuretic. Midol™ is a common commercial anti-cramping medication. Anti-cramping medications, since they deal specific with a condition experienced only by women, should by extension, only be located in common areas or in women's rooms. It may seem silly to mention, however, I have seen this rule disregarded. Depending on your supplier, you should expect to buy this medication for about $.30 per unit with a retail price of $.75-$1.00.

Bandages

Scrapes and cuts happen in life. Selling bandages through mechanical vending machines can be a great answer to this problem. These bandages are sold through cardboard packages like condoms or OTC medications. You can purchase prepackaged bandages or pack them yourself. This can help keep your costs low and your profit margins high.

Golf Balls

Although they are not nearly as common as the other types of products that are described in this work, golf balls can also be sold through bulk vending machines. There are specially made bulk vending machines that are designed with golf balls in mind. Additionally, I have even heard reports that golf balls can be sold through 2 inch capsule machines, although these have not been confirmed. This might be something worth considering if you already have a golf course or driving range on your route. This is especially true of a course that has limited retail sales available. You can always ask. Machines can easily be set to charge $1.00 for balls.

Fish/Duck/Animal Food

This machine which is loaded with corn is located at a petting zoo. This type of setup is also common at fish farms and duck ponds.

Another use for bulk vending machines, other than candy, is to dispense feed that is used to attract animals. This sort of setup is common at petting zoos, nature walks, duck ponds and fish ponds. All that is done instead of filling the machine with candy, it is filled with the feed in question. This feed is usually just crude protein, fat and fiber and is very inexpensive. Charging just a quarter for a handful of fish food can be very profitable.

Conclusion

In the pages of this chapter, we have discussed many different types of bulk vending products. These will make up the vast majority of any products that you offer on your route. These items are time tested and have been proven both reliable and profitable. Do not, however, limit yourself to these products alone. Keep your eyes open for new products and listen to what your customers are looking for.

Chapter 4
Bulk Vending Inventory Management

Without product in your machines, you will have nothing to sell and will not make any money. This means, that you need make sure that you keep a well stocked supply of candies and other products to feed your business. However, as a business person with a sharp eye to the bottom line, you also need to make sure that you shop around and get the lowest possible price for your product. In the sections that follow, we will discuss determining the costs of the products you sell, tracking sales and the options that you will have as to where you can buy your products. We will also discuss the advantages and disadvantages that each of these product suppliers has to offer.

Bulk Vending Is All About Weight

Bulk vending, the business of selling loose candy and food through mechanical vending machines, is all about weight. You will not buy or sell candy by the piece, but instead buy and sell it by pounds or kilograms and sell it in grams or ounces. You will need to understand weights and be comfortable applying them to your inventory management.

The basics of weight are fairly simple, but I will go through them here quickly to make sure we are all on the same page. In the United States, the primary unit of measuring weight is the pound (abbreviated "lb."). This is part of the British Imperial System (ironically, even the British no longer use this system). A pound is in turn made up of sixteen ounces, which is abbreviated ".oz". Another common unit of measuring weight (actually the standard everywhere else in the world) is the kilogram. A kilogram is heavier than a pound weighing approximately 2.2 pounds. The kilogram is abbreviated with the symbol "kg". A kilogram is subdivided into 1000 grams, which are abbreviated "g".

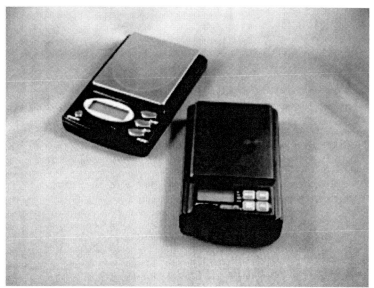

Small digital scales are inexpensive and are very helpful in determining the cost of the goods you are selling.

Some scales will also be very helpful in the bulk vending aspect of your business. It would be wise to invest in both a bathroom scale, as well as the pocket scales shown above. These will be very useful in determining the cost of vending a product. Also, to take stock of a bulk candy/food inventory, you will need to weigh the product you have on hand. The bathroom scale will be invaluable for doing this.

Costs Per Vend

One of the most important activities that you can carry out as a bulk vendor is determining the costs of the products you are vending. Without a thorough understanding of the true cost of a product, you cannot determine what is called marginal profit, that is the profit made from selling one single item.

The cost per vend is simply the amount of money that must be spent to provide the amount of product that is sold through one vend of a machine. Determining the cost per vend is very simple as long as you have one of the small scales that were just discussed. The process is this:

- ✓ Load up a machine with the product whose cost per vend you want to determine.
- ✓ Vend the machine three times. Each time, remove the product and set it aside in separate piles.
- ✓ Weigh each pile using the digital scale using ounces if the product is sold by the pound, or grams if the product is sold by the kilogram.
- ✓ Take the average of the three weights. To take an average, add the three weights together and divide by 3. For example, .3 oz., .5oz, and .4 oz, add up to 1.2 oz. Dividing this by three provides an average weight of .4 oz.
- ✓ Divide the average weight by 16 if the product is sold by the pound or 1000 if the product is sold by the kilogram. Write this number down. For example .4 / 16 = .025 .
- ✓ Multiply the cost of a pound or kilogram of product by the number found in step 5. For example (.025 x $2.50) = $.06.

The number found in step 6 of the process listed above is the average cost per vend of the product in question. In this example, the cost of selling one vend worth of product is six cents. If you are selling the product for twenty five cents, you know that you have a gross profit of nineteen cents every time the machine knob is turned.

Defining Marginal Profit

Profit is the name of the game in business. Simply put, profit is the money that you make carrying out a business activity. However, there are two types of profit that you should understand in business. The first of these is gross profit.

Marginal profit, is the amount of profit you make from selling one more unit. In the case of bulk vending, this is the profit from a single vend. You should know the marginal profit (just as much as cost) of each product you sell.

To determine the marginal profit of a particular candy (or any item for that matter) you simply subtract the cost (like we determined in the last section) from the sale price of any item. For example, say you sell some candy for $.50 with a cost of $.10 per vend. In this case, your marginal profit would be $.50-$.10 or $.40.

From this information, you know that every time you vend a portion of that candy, your company is making $.40. This type of information will be invaluable when setting prices and deciding what candies to carry. Do you sell the one that has a marginal profit of $.20 or the one with a marginal profit of $.40? Easy answer.

Tracking Sales & Expenses

It is absolutely crucial that you track the sales of each machine that your business operates over time. This information will help you to determine if machines are becoming more popular, or if a new product you have introduced is a better seller. Over time this information can become very useful. You will see patterns emerge, and if you ever want to sell your route, this information will be very interesting to any prospective buyers and may result in a higher price for your route.

There are many ways that you can track these sales. The easiest way is to go and buy a notebook and write everything down. This is a time tested and simple way to record business information. Simply write down how much money you collect from each machine and when you collect it.

If you prefer to track everything on a computer, you can do that as well. The easiest way to track everything on a computer is with the use of a computerized spreadsheet program. These are available with any office application suite and are pretty easy to use once you get the hang of them. There is a great free office program out there called OpenOffice. This program can be downloaded for free and used without a license by going to www.openoffice.org. The suite includes a very robust spreadsheet program called Calc.

There are also software programs out there that will help you keep track of a mechanical vending business. These use databases and sophisticated interfaces to make managing information simple. These do range in cost a bit so do your homework before you buy a program. One good idea is to take advantage of any free trial offers. This will allow you to evaluate the product before you commit any money.

Bulk Vending Supply Sources

Grocery Bulk

The easiest place to buy product for a bulk route is probably the bulk section of a local grocery store. Many grocery stores stock all kinds of candy and other food that will work well in bulk machines.

Bulk grocery bins, such as these, can provide a convenient, if not slightly expensive, source of product.

The advantage of purchasing from the bulk section of a grocery store is convenience. You can purchase any amount of product that you want, from a single piece of candy well beyond fifty pounds. Additionally, these stores can even be open 24 hours a day. This means that no matter what time of day, or even the day of the year, you can quickly lay your hands on any product that is needed. In many of these bulk sections, you can even find specialty candies and foods that may be difficult to find through other suppliers. A typical example of this is specialty candies from Mexico.

There are disadvantages to buying in a bulk store as well. Firstly, you will need to develop a sanitary storage system for the items that you buy in a bulk grocery section. The bags that you buy everything in will not work in the long term. Inexpensive plastic (food grade) storage containers will work. Secondly, you will tend to pay a higher amount per pound for the candy. After all, you are not really buying in a wholesale lot, but instead are paying lower cost retail. Both of these facts make buying from a grocery bulk section, an option of last resort. You should really use this option, when you are in a pinch for product and are worrying more about availability rather than cost.

Wholesale Stores

Across America in the last 20 years there has been an explosion of wholesale stores and clubs. Large retail chains have even developed their own chains based on the principle of "buy in bulk and save". In addition to the wholesale price clubs that cater to consumers, there are also wholesale grocery stores that cater to businesses. Frequently, when, say a restaurant, runs out of burger buns, they will turn to one of these stores to fill the gap until their next supply delivery occurs. These business oriented wholesale stores can have an even better selection of bulk vending product than their consumer oriented counterparts.

These stores can be an excellent source of product to sell through your bulk vending machines. They offer excellent selections, convenient hours, and replenish their inventories throughout the day. Due to the bulk buying concept of these stores, you will also receive better pricing than you would at a retail grocery store. This means a higher profit margin and a more profitable bottom line for your company.

One of the downsides of a wholesale store is that they will not offer the non-food products that have been discussed such as condoms, stickers, or non-prescription drugs. For these you will have to rely on specialty vending suppliers. Other than that, the only other downside is that some of these stores will charge an annual membership fee. If at all possible, avoid paying fees to keep your costs low. However, if your bulk vending route sells candy and other foods exclusively, a wholesale store can easily answer all of your supply needs.

Online Suppliers

The Internet is one of the best resources that exists today for finding products. No matter what type of product that you are in search of, be it stickers, candy, condoms, non-prescription drugs, toys, jewelry, novelties, capsules, etc, the Internet is will offer many suppliers at very competitive prices. In most cases, all you will need to do is conduct a search using a search engine. Something simple such as "bulk vending candy" alone will generate many suppliers ready willing and able to do business with you.

Internet business will be carried out through the mail. This adds the cost of shipping the product to your profit equation. Always remember to take shipping into account when comparing costs between internet suppliers and suppliers in your home town. It is not impossible that a wholesale store can still deliver the lowest price. This may be because these stores deal in very large purchases and have streamlined logistics divisions that can compete with and even beat the cost of private mail shippers.

Lastly, when doing business through the Internet, always be wary of unreliable suppliers and scams. Since almost all internet business is carried out through the mail, you will have limited recourse in the event that your product does not arrive or arrives late or damaged. Consider starting small with an internet supplier to gauge their service. If you are pleased, you can always order more. However, if you are unhappy with the service or do not receive your order, you will not be out that much money.

One way that you can avoid the risk of scams or unreliability is by using auction and sales sites like eBay.com (www.ebay.com) and Amazon (www.amazon.com). These services are powerhouses of internet commerce. Both have strong rating and feedback systems in place to make sure that bad sellers are quickly removed. Both also offer guarantees that what you order will be what you receive. For more information and the most up to date info concerning these guarantees, consult these fine retailers.

Bulk Vending Distributors

If you live in a large city, there is a good chance that there is a specialized business that distributes candy and other food products to convenience stores, gas stations, bodegas and other smaller retail stores. These companies may be of use to you in procuring candy and other food items to sell in your machines.

Specialty distributors can be very useful in supplying you with product to sell in your machines. They will often have whole warehouses full of product.

The phone book, and more recently, internet phone directories, will be the best and most convenient place to find these distributors. Additionally, the distribution companies that supply restaurants and bars with such items as peanuts may also be a source that is worth exploring.

If you live in one of the large metropolitan areas of your state, you may be fortunate enough to have a specialized vending distributor who maintains a warehouse close to your area of operation. Make every effort to find these businesses by speaking with other vending operators and vending machine retailers in your area. They will most often be happy to point you in the right direction. In some cases, machine suppliers will also be product distributors. The search will be worth your time. Specialized vending distributors will frequently offer the absolute best selection in town, on a level with internet distributors. However, since they are local, you will not have to pay to ship. This can significantly lower your costs and increase your bottom line.

Distributors are great for selection, and because of the levels of inventory they carry, can frequently offer the best prices around. You may need to establish an account with them before they will let you purchase though. This is not a terribly complicated step, but if you are a small operator, may be more headache than you want to deal with. If that is the case, the wholesale stores are your best bet for candy. Any specialty items will need to be purchased online most likely. If you do want establish an account, it might be worth it, depending on how large you want to grow. Some distributors will even offer convenient lines of credit and flexible billing, on approved credit of course.

Expiration Dates, Spoilage and Waste Tracking

In the event that items have reached their expiration date or have melted or otherwise spoiled, remove them from the machine or warehouse immediately. You do not want these being sold to customers. You will need to account for these items on what is termed a "waste sheet". This sheet will help you track the amount of product that was lost to spoilage. These items will need to be accounted for and replaced in inventory.

You will also be able to determine what types of items are susceptible to spoilage and how they were lost. Armed with this information, you can help to keep product waste low. This only increases the profitability of your operation.

Storing Your Product

Storing your product is one of the biggest inventory management challenges that you will face when operating a bulk vending business. Wherever you store your product will need to be both cool and dry. Heat can easily cause melting and the spoilage of product. Heat can also cause the degradation of latex for condoms as well. Moisture is a terrible enemy to food products and can cause molding and be hazardous to the health of your customers as well. If moisture is a problem, consider buying a dehumidifier,

You will also need to make sure that your product is raised off the floor. This, again, is a health and safety concern. Flooding can again cause spoilage and the floor is not a sanitary surface. Raising your product several inches will prevent this from being a problem.

There are two solutions that will answer all of these problems and offer you a headache free storage system. These are shelving and storage cabinets.

Metro shelving like this, which can be used to make shelving that fits any need or situation, can be very convenient to a vending operation.

Wire frame metro shelving is an excellent choice for your product storage needs. This type of shelving is very sturdy and can easily support the weight of all your product. Additionally, this type of shelving is sold in pieces. The poles are sold separately from the shelves. This means that a shelving system can be customized to fit any space. Many different sizes of shelves are available, as well as pole sizes. Additionally, you can add locking wheeled casters to the bases of the poles for easy movement. Commercial grade metro shelving is a great choice, but is a little expensive when compared with other options. A complete four shelf system that is 5' tall will often cost about $200. However, the higher cost of this equipment will pay for itself with years of reliable service.

In addition to wire metro shelving, steel frame "rivet-rak" shelving can be another great selection for storing and organizing product. This shelving system incorporates steel frame supports and shelves, with the shelves themselves being made of particle board. The shelves lock into the steel frame with four metal rivets at each corner. This creates a very strong and very sturdy shelf.

This type of shelving system is sold in a complete kit so you will need to know the exact space you have available before ordering. Of course, as well, you will need to keep the particle boards dry or they will fall apart. However, these shelf systems are a little less expensive than metro shelving, can be assembled in minutes with minimal tools and will serve a young business well for years.

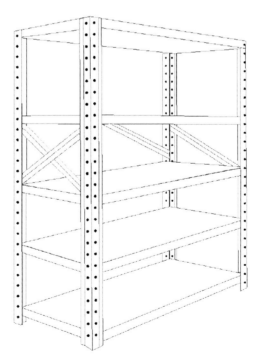

Rivet rack style shelving looks like the above picture. These rack systems are sturdy and fairly inexpensive.

Shelving is a great system for storing your product; however, a cabinet offers some advantages shelving does not. For example, a cabinet has a door that can be locked. This can help keep children, roommates, visitors, or employees from helping themselves to product whenever the mood strikes. Trust me, if you store a lot of candy in a home with children, candy will disappear over time, and with it potential profits. A lock can go a long way to eliminating this problem.

There are many types of cabinets that will work to store your product. The simplest is a plywood cabinet kit. Kits of this type can be purchased in hardware and general merchandise stores. The wholesale stores described earlier will undoubtedly sell them. These can be assembled with a few household tools in less than half an hour. The addition of a padlock hasp (many kits include these) will provide a secure place to store product over the years.

Mini Storage Parks

It is entirely possible to base a bulk vending business in your home. The space requirements of the machines, equipment and any office equipment tend to be fairly small. However, this is not to say that you will not need more space. Families grow and house sizes range, so it is entirely possible that your home will not be able to offer you or your business the room it will need to grow.

Mini storage lockers, such as these can offer a convenient location to store your machines, product and even vehicles.

If that is the case, a mini storage locker makes an excellent home for your operation. Most likely you are familiar with these parks. In exchange for a monthly rental fee, you will receive a locking space to store whatever you wish. Sizes range from 10 to 400 square feet and you can always adjust based on your needs. The extra security of a locking space can be very handy. Additionally, these parks have locking gates as well as camera monitoring. The peace of mind that your investment and business are safe 24 hours a day can be worth the monthly rent.

Additionally, and I am not a tax preparer or attorney, you may be able to write of the monthly rent of a storage space as a business expense on your annual taxes. Check with a licensed accountant or tax preparer for the most current and relevant information.

Rent for a storage locker varies with the size of the unit. However, rents usually start from about $25. You will need to fill out an application as well as pay the first month in advance. One other concern when storing product and equipment in a mini storage park is the environment. You need to make sure that the temperatures do not exceed or fall below the safe handling temperatures of your product. The added benefit of convenience and more space can quickly be destroyed by the costs associated with product spoilage.

Experimenting To Find What Sells

It is important that you are flexible in your product selection. It is a good idea to start off a new location with a good mix of products. For example, say you have just placed a new bulk vending machine with four product compartments in a hair salon. It would be a bad idea to simply stock all four of those compartments with chocolate candy right from the start. Who knows what people in the salon like? If you only offer one selection, you will not be able to gauge their reaction and develop an insight into their wants and habits. If on the other hand, you start off with a mix of one chocolate, one fruit candy, one salty snack (like peanuts) and maybe some sort of spicy sweet cinnamon candy, you will have a better idea of what the clientele wants simply by seeing which items are selling.

This same spirit of experimentation should also apply to removing poor sellers and replacing them with better ones. I have had locations in the past, where I could not sell one type of product to save my life. Finally, I just gave up and pulled it. When I replaced the bad selling product with a new line, I could not keep it in stock. Through the experimentation, I found a winner. Don't be afraid to employ this same tactic. A little playing around can find an ideal product mix that really will increase sales.

Conclusion

Managing your inventory will be one of the most critical tasks that you perform as a bulk vending operator. You need to make sure to offer an inventory of products at prices that they will pay. You need to keep you expenses as low as possible to make sure your business is making as much money as it can. Also, you need to make sure that you have an efficient storage system in place to protect your products from spoilage and waste. If you can effectively manage your inventory, most of the hard work of being a bulk vending operator is already done.

Chapter 5
Finding Locations & Installation

In Vending Machine Fundamentals, I discussed many different ways to go about finding locations for your new vending business. All of these methods can be used to find locations for a bulk vending business as well. I would not, however, recommend any kind of cash sign up bonus like those I described in the first volume of this series. These are really only appropriate to full service vending, and you will find it a long time indeed before you recoup your money.

Consider Bulk Vending Sponsorship

Sponsorship is an extremely useful and necessary tool to a bulk vending operator.

This is how it works. You, as a bulk vending operator, contact and apply to participate in the vending program of a participating charity. When you are enrolled in the program, you will be able to purchase stickers that you can place on your machines. For the use of these stickers, you will pay a monthly fee to the particular charity that issued them. With some charities, you have the option to pay a lump sum annual fee at a slightly reduced rate. These fees vary, but are very reasonable and average about $1.50 per month, per sticker. These fees add up quickly and many charities have been able to raise money on an annual basis to continue their good work.

Along with helping to fund the works of these charities, these stickers also provide exposure for the charities to the public. With a missing child they may turn up in a school across the country. What if a young person is buying a gumball or a sticker, and sees the face of one of their classmates? Perhaps they will point this out to an adult and help to recover the child for their guardian.

Additionally, these stickers provide your business with an added incentive for location managers to accept your machines. When you say that the placement of a machine helps to fund a charity, who can say no? Often, if you say you would like to place a machine at a location and say that it will help to sponsor a specific charity, the owner may not even bring up the notion of commission or will waive it.

To sign up for a program, you will need to contact a charity. They should be able to provide you with a comprehensive information packet. In this packet will be an application and a business agreement. Read these documents through carefully. They will spell out your responsibilities in the program. You will need to adhere to these strictly.

Any way that you slice it, you should strongly consider participating in one of the available charity vending programs. Programs are frequently added to the list of vending charities. The easiest way to find one of these charities is to look on the internet using a search engine. The search string "Vending Sticker Program" will yield good and current results. If at all possible find a local charity.

Walk And Talk

One of the best and easiest ways to find locations for a bulk vending route is to simply start visiting businesses in person. It is not uncommon to target a certain neighborhood, take some machines with you in your car, and just start pounding the pavement. This is especially easy to do with bulk vending machines, because the business owners can immediately see the machine, and you can place it in minutes.

This sort of operation is all about the sales pitch, and a face to face meeting is often much more effective than cold bulk mail campaigns or phone calls. It is easy to throw a letter in the recycling; it is much more uncomfortable to refuse an actual person. This is made even harder when you are working with a charity and your machines help to support those operations. Not many people will say no to a charity.

When you go on "walk and talks", make sure you set the right tone from the start. First and foremost, make sure that you are dressed appropriately. Dressing business casual is a good place to start. A button up shirt and slacks is really all you need. Leave any ties in the closet. Next, make sure your personal hygiene is up to par. Essentially, you are interviewing for the job of vendor at each business you stop at, so dress the part.

It is also helpful to take some props along with you that will convey an air of professionalism. A business portfolio aids in this effort nicely. It looks professional, and may help you keep from fidgeting while you work up your salesman confidence. Also, business cards are a good idea for this kind of sales pitch. Many times, the boss may be out, or will need to ask the permission of the owner, if they do and get approval to place a machine, you want them to have all of your contact information.

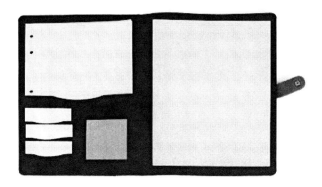

A business portfolio is an essential tool, when cold calling, that adds an air of professionalism and keeps your hands busy.

There is no reason whatsoever that you cannot take machines with you in the car when you go on walk and talks. In fact, I would strongly recommend it. You should also have product with you as well. This way, when you get the green light to place a machine on location, you can just go get on out of the car and have it set up in 15 minutes.

It is also a great idea to set goals when you go on walk and talks. For example, tell yourself that you want to set up two locations when you first start for the day. Or, I will talk to fifteen businesses today. Work at it and meet your goal, whatever it is. Once you have, you can finish for the day. In sales situations like this, goals and quotas help keep you on track and help to deflect the inevitable rejection that you will get. Remember to just keep at it and meet your goal.

Buying Existing Routes

Bulk vending businesses are fairly inexpensive to start. A small investment of $3,000 can readily be turned into a business of 20+ machines on location producing revenue. This creates another opportunity that was not discussed in length in my last book, Vending Machine Fundamentals.

Often, a bulk vending machine operator will decide to leave the business for one reason or another. Retirees are common operators of bulk vending routes. They may start a small business to help transition into retired life and give them some revenue on the side. At some point, they decide that they do not need the headaches of owning a small business (jammed coin mechanisms, stolen machines, etc.) and decide that they want out. Other times, people will decide that, after some consideration, they do not have the time necessary to devote to a business and take care of their families and one has to go. This can create a great opportunity for someone who wants to get into the vending business.

Essentially, these people have done all of the hard work in getting the machines on location, figuring out which product to sell, and establishing a customer base. When you buy a route, all you really need to do is keep things humming along and take the profits. Due to this, buying a complete route can be great. Additionally, someone who is selling their whole route can often be a motivated seller. This may allow you to purchase the route for less than it would cost you to build one on your own. Often, they will simply want to recoup the money that was spent on the machines, and will not ask anything for all of their time and energy.

You will need to exercise some good judgment and caution when buying a complete route. The first thing that you will need to do is meet the seller. Get a good sense of them. Make sure that you feel comfortable dealing with them. You also will need to go and inspect **EVERY** machine that is on location. Do this with the seller. Have them open the machine for you and allow you to inspect it. This will take some time, but will almost guarantee that they own the machines.

I know an operator who fell in with a less than reliable character when they were first getting started. This person was supposedly selling some machines on location. When the new operator went to look at them without the "seller", they were met with suspicion. The business owner called the real owner/operator of the machines and handed the phone to the interested buyer. The owner/operator had no idea who this person was that was supposedly selling the machines. He was a little angry, but the new vendor assured them that it was an honest mistake and they were the near victim of a fraud. When the new operator tried to call the "seller" back, the number had been disconnected. This is not a common fraud, but can happen. Fortunately in this case, no money had changed hands. If the guys in that warehouse had not been suspicious and made a phone call, the new vendor could have been cheated out of a lot of money. Always be cautious.

Also, make sure you speak to the managers as was discussed in the last section and make sure that the change of ownership is ok with them.

A Few Words On Bulk Vending Commissions

It is not uncommon in the vending business for you to share the proceeds of bulk vending machines with the business owner. After all, without their location and customers, you would not be able to make any money.

Now, it is always a good policy to not bring up commissions until the location owner or manager does. They may not want anything for allowing the machine placement, they may view the machine as a valuable service for their customers. In fact, often times you will be asked is there is a cost to the location for placing the machine. That means they think they need to pay you!

If commissions are brought up, it is best that you have a plan ready to go so you will not get caught unprepared and make an offer that is bad for your business or will cost you money. So, a little thought ahead of time can be very valuable. You may decide that any commission is too much and any location that asks for one should be passed over. It is your business. You decide what is best.

Common commission rates for full service locations run from about 10%-25%. That is under a situation where the gross profit potential is 100% or so. With bulk vending, it is common for commission rates to approach 25%-50% of the gross amount in the machine. Since bulk vending has higher profit potentials, a higher commission rate is not inappropriate.

Remember; don't bring up commissions until they do. It is often much easier and profitable for you to rely on charity sponsorship (see next section) to get in the door, but if the location wants a cut keep it as low as possible to secure the location. Don't give away the store.

If you do decide to offer a commission, it is a good idea to divide up the money when you service the machine. Count the money and give the location their cut right then and there. I have known vendors who would send a check at the end of the month. However, checks cost money and there is a lack of transparency that can breed mistrust. Save yourself the headache and just divide the money then and there and give it to the location, even if it is all quarters.

Turn-Key Bulk Vending Routes

If the idea of buying a complete vending business that is ready made with locations, machines, and inventory appeals to you, than a turn-key bulk vending route might be right for you.

There are companies out there that specialize in this exact type of service. The sell machines as their main business, however, to make it easier and convenient for you to buy their machines, they will help you put together a route in your area.

These companies work with vending machine locators (discussed in *Vending Machine Fundamentals: How To Build Your Own Route*) to place machines and then sell you the whole package for a set price. Usually, you will pay for the machine and a separate fee for the locating service. Routes such as these are commonly sold in groups of 20 or more. Financing is also commonly available.

With this type of service, since much of the work is being done for you, you will pay a higher price then you would building your own route. However, this does appeal to some people who hate the idea of selling themselves and their services and want the hard work taken care of. If you are one of these people, and there is nothing wrong with that, this is an option you should consider.

One word of caution is appropriate. Not everyone in this world is an honest person. Make sure that the person or company with whom you are dealing is legitimate before sending out any checks. Do your homework and check them out before it is too late and you have learned an expensive business lesson. Ask for references from other satisfied customers and if they cannot be provided, be very skeptical. As with everything in life, buyer beware!

48 Hour Installation Time

When operating a full service vending route that incorporates heavy soda and snack machines, machine installation on location can be quite an ordeal. These machines can weight many hundreds of pounds and require specialized moving trucks, utility hand trucks and even pallet jacks to move them. These machines cannot even be moved by a single person, but should be moved by a team. All of these factors can cause a delay in the amount of time that is required to place a machine on location. With full service vending, 1-2 weeks is a common amount of time to wait for a machine to be installed.

Although rack systems may require moving trucks and assistants, the vast majority of bulk vending machines can be moved without them. In fact, in most cases you will not need anything more than your own two arms and your current vehicle. This means that you can quickly install machines on location.

As a business owner, you need to set a reasonable goal for the amount of time it will take you to have a machine on location. 48 hours is a reasonable amount of time, and should not be exceeded. If this amount of time, between when you get permission to put a machine on location and when it is installed, is exceeded, you run the risk of looking unprofessional and loosing the new account. As a business owner, this should be avoided at all costs.

Marking Your Machines

As a vending machine owner, it will be your responsibility to make sure all of your new business' property is identified as belonging to your company. There are two ways that this can be done.

A property sticker is a label that is affixed to the machine in a prominent spot. It tells the customers of the machine, as well as the employees and the manager of the machine location, who the machine belongs to. In addition to the name of the business, all relevant contact information should be included. Most importantly, this is a phone number, but these days can also include an email. It is not absolutely necessary that you include an address. Often, when operating a bulk vending business, you will operate from your home. It is entirely reasonable that you will not want people dropping by unannounced to talk about vending machines.

You will want to make sure that the labels you use are of a high quality. You do not want to print out cheap labels on your home printer. The adhesives on these labels can quickly fade and the labels may fall off. Additionally, labels printed on a home printer can smudge and become illegible. If either of these two things happens, the location manager or unhappy customers will not know how to reach you. This is bad. A print shop can easily print labels that will not smudge and will remain in place on your machines.

Labels are intended to be a professional, visible means to let your customers know how to get in contact with you in the event there is a problem with a vending machine. However, labels can be removed. If your machines do not have serial numbers, there is no way for you to distinguish one machine from the next. If you wish to more permanently mark your machines, in the absence of a serial number, you will need to use an engraver.

An engraver is a specialized high speed power tool that can be used to etch writing onto suitable materials such as metal and plastic. Engraving should not be used in place of property stickers, but only as a discreet way to permanently mark your machines. If someone steals a machine and walks it into a pawn shop, an engraving on the bottom of the machine (out of sight in normal use) may alert the pawnbroker that the machine is stolen. They in turn may call the police and you may get your machine back.

A common rotary tool like this one can be used to engrave your machines in a permanent manner.

Wall Mounting

Some of the machines that you may choose to add to your route will need to be hung on a wall, like the one pictured on page 30. This is often the most convenient place for the machine to be located, as well as one of the strongest methods for securing your machine. With some of the hardware listed on the next pages, it would be almost impossible to remove the machine without taking the wall with it!

Before you ever attempt to mount a wall to a machine, do your homework first. Know what type of material you will be affixing the machine to. You will need to bring the proper hardware as well as appropriate tools for the wall material. Additionally, know what is behind the wall. It is never a good thing to run a drill bit into an electrical conduit or pipe. This can cause thousands of dollars in damage, for which you would be liable. **If you do not know what you are doing, seek professional advice or hire a professional to mount the machine for you.**

If you decide to mount the machine yourself, take a second person along. Although the machines that you are mounting to the wall may seem light, they become very heavy and impossible to hang if you are trying to hold the machine up with one hand and precisely mount the machine with a power tool in the other hand. A second set of eyes will also be useful in making sure the machine is level. It is really just much easier to have help.

The right tools are also an absolute must. A drill will be required for mounting to a wall. If you are mounting to a solid concrete, brick or concrete block wall, you will need a hammer drill. This type of drill moves the bit forward at high rates to help pulverize the material that is being drilled. This has the effect of cutting down the drilling time dramatically. If you are mounting the machine to a hollow wall a stud finder will also be a necessary tool. This tool uses magnetism to detect the 2x4's or studs that make up the support system in the wall. It is much more sturdy to mount a machine to one of these studs instead of just to the drywall itself. Along with a drill and a stud finder, you should take a level. This tool will be helpful in making sure that the machine is mounted in a level fashion. There is nothing worse that working for an hour, sweating, to mount a machine and then realizing that it is crooked. Lastly, bring a pencil. This tool will be used to mark the walls, but can quickly be wiped away without any permanent damage.

Installation Hardware

To mount a machine to a wall, you will need to use the right hardware. As was stated earlier, each job is different, if you are unsure how to proceed, consult a professional, or hire them to do the job for you. It is not worth the risk of hurting yourself or damaging the location.

In this section, a variety of types of mounting hardware will be presented. Each of these has specific uses for which they are designed. Always use each type of hardware as the manufacturer instructs and make sure that the hardware is sufficient for the load that it will need to bear. For information, including video examples of how to use these types of hardware, you can often consult the internet or the hardware manufacturer's website.

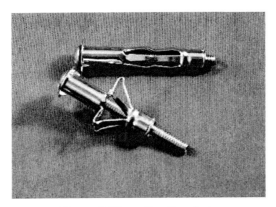

Drywall Mounting Brackets

Drywall mounting brackets are used to mount something to the drywall of a hollow wall. This type of hardware is a steel tube before it is used. A hole is drilled and the bracket is inserted into the hole. When the screw inside the cylinder is turned clockwise, the cylinder is crushed and forced to expand outwards as shown in the picture above. This creates a large bracket inside of the wall. Also, the weight of the load placed on the screw will be distributed over a larger space of the drywall making it much stronger. Once the cylinder has been crushed, the screw can be easily removed to hang the machine. However, the crushed cylinder can be hard if not impossible to remove from the wall, short of cutting it out.

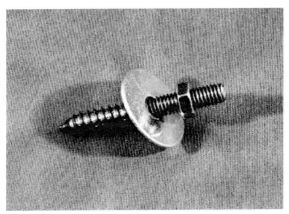

Hanger Bolt

A hanger bolt is a double edged screw that is used to mount items into the studs of a hollow wall. For this purpose, a hanger bolt has two different types of threads on it. The first end is a pointed, wood screw. This is the end that is fixed into the stud in the wall. To do this, you will need to use a stud finder, and drill the appropriate sized hole for the hanger bolt you are using (see manufacturer's instructions). Once the wood screw is in place, the machine screw end of the bolt will protrude from the wall. With the correct number of these, you can hang the machine and bolt it securely in place using washers and a machine nut.

Sleeve anchors are used to mount machines into brick or concrete block. The bolt is inserted through the metal tube (this is the sleeve and gives this hardware its name). The washer is placed over the threaded end of the bole and the nut is screwed into place. The unit is then placed in an appropriately prepared and sized hole in the concrete block or brick wall. As the nut is tightened, the wedge end of the bolt forces the sleeve to expand into the sides of the hole in the wall. This creates tremendous pressure that makes it almost impossible to remove the anchor without loosening the bolt.

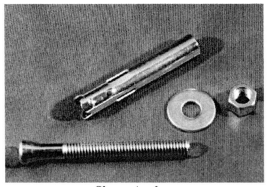

Sleeve Anchor

Wedge anchors are used to secure equipment to a concrete floor. This is the type of anchor that would be used to secure a floor safe, ATM or a cabinet style vending machine. This piece of hardware works in a very similar manner to the sleeve anchor, in that as the nut is tightened; the wedge end of the bolt forcefully expands a metal ring into the sides of the hole. This again, creates tremendous pressure that makes it all but impossible to remove the equipment, without first removing the bolts.

Wedge Anchor

Drop in anchors are another popular type of hardware that can be used to fasten items to concrete. Again, using a predrilled hole, the anchor is inserted into the concrete. Then, by threading the bolt into the anchor, the anchor is expanded into the sides of the hole. Again, the tremendous pressure that is created will hold the load in place. Again, make sure you adhere to all manufacturers' specifications.

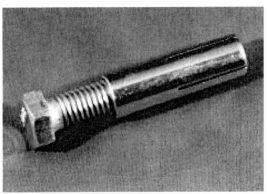
Drop-in Anchor

Conclusion

Finding locations for your machines can be the biggest challenge that you face as a new vendor. The pages in this chapter have given you all the information you need to find these locations. There will be rejection. This is natural. Stay with it, and remain focused and determined, and there is no reason that you will not find those locations in time. Just remember to be patient and keep motivated.

Chapter 6
Servicing A Bulk Route

Business Is Based On Relationships

Business is all about relationships. Never forget this. This is the most important section in this book. You will find that over time, the people and businesses that you want to deal with are the ones that are friendly and generally concerned about you as a customer. This will be true of the businesses where you place machines as well. They will want you to be service oriented, friendly, professional and courteous. Always work hard to protect these relationships and your company's reputation. You will never lose out by doing so.

Servicing A Bulk Vending Location

Servicing a bulk vending machine on location is not a terribly difficult process. However, I am a big fan of checklists, and I decided one would be good to help keep a new vendor organized. When servicing a machine, you need to:

- Visually inspect the machine.
- Open the lock and remove all money.
- Open the product compartment and inspect the product.
- Fill product as necessary (remember new product goes on top).
- Test vend the machine (this makes sure there are no coin jams).
- If everything is working fine, lock the product and money compartments.
- Clean the exterior of the machine to eliminate fingerprints and stickiness.
- Check the property sticker and make sure it does not need to be replaced. These often get peeled off or fade over time.
- Talk to the location manager if possible or the employees. Make sure there are no problems and everything is good. This would be when you count money and provide commission if you have a commission agreement.

This list may seem simple and basic, but following it each and every time will ensure happy customers, happy business owners and a profitable machine.

Bulk Vending Service Schedules

Soda and snack vending machines, in high volume locations, can require lots of servicing. From past experience, I know that soda machines in the peak of summer can even require daily servicing! This can lead to lots of profit, as well as a significant time commitment. This makes full size vending quite unsuitable for many working people. This is not true for bulk vending machines, however.

Bulk vending machines will require considerably less time in servicing than the larger full size machines. This is what makes them attractive as an extra source of income. It is not uncommon for bulk vendors to service their machines on a monthly basis. This is due to the fact that bulk vending machines incur a slower, although more profitable, sales rate than full size machines.

A good place to start once you have established your bulk route is a two week cycle. This means that you show up to service your machines every two weeks. Depending on the level of business that you receive, you can always adjust your service frequency. If you find that your machines are always picked clean when you arrive, you can switch to a weekly cycle. If on the other hand, there is hardly any money in the machines when you arrive, consider switching to a monthly schedule. Either way, be flexible and adapt as needed.

Coin Management

The machines that are described in this book accept only coins. There are bulk style machines that can accept dollar bills, but these machines require a capital investment and technical expertise that is beyond the scope of this book. This means that all of the money that you collect from machines is going to be in the form of quarters. This means, that as part of both your machine servicing routine, you will need to develop procedures and practices for dealing with the money that you remove from machines.

When you first open a machine, you will need to remove the money. After all, this is what building a bulk vending business is all about. It is quite natural to get a kick the first time you open a machine and find it full of money that was not there before. Enjoy it. It is a good idea to keep the money from each machine, if not each selection (if the machine is a multiple select) separate. Additionally, mark which money came from which machine and which product type.

Money bags such as these are very handy for keeping cash safe while servicing machines.

Many vendors like to use money bags like the ones shown above to keep money safe and contained while servicing a route. You can take this even further by using zip lock plastic bags to keep coins from intermingling.

It is important to keep money from different machines and selections separate for the purposes of tracking your business' growth. If you simply threw every coin into one bag and did not separate them (many new vendors do this and it is a mistake) you could not tell if sales are increasing, decreasing or plateauing for a particular product or a specific machine. If, on the other hand you did keep monies separate, you can tell all of this and make much more informed business decisions with this information.

When you return to your home base, you will need to count the money. You will also most likely need to roll the coins as well. Anyone who has ever counted large amounts of coin can tell you it can be a tedious process that can quickly become a chore. To help with counting the coins, there are tools that you can purchase. The most basic and inexpensive of these is a coin counter, like the one shown below.

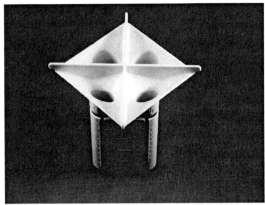

A simple plastic coin counter is an inexpensive way to make counting all of your coins much easier.

Coin counters are simply plastic tubes with a funnel top into which you dump sorted coins (quarters into one, nickels another, etc.). These tools can be found for under $10 in most office supply stores. I strongly recommend buying one. The tubes of the coins will fill up to preset intervals of $10 for quarters, $5 for dimes, $2 for nickels and $.50 for pennies.

The use of a coin counters requires that you separate the coins into individual piles. Since almost all coins will be quarters, this should be easy. If you wish to avoid even this, you can buy an electronic coin counter. These machines, a smaller version of the kind used by banks, can count hundreds of coins a minute and display the tally on a convenient LCD display. In my opinion, these are unnecessary pieces of equipment for a bulk vendor. In reality most of the coins you will get will be quarters anyway, and the $200 a coin counter can cost would be better spent on another machine to put on location.

Once you have counted the coins, you will need to take them to a bank and have them deposited into your account.

Key Management

It may seem like a small matter, but to an experienced vendor, keeping track of all the keys that you will need to run your business can be quite a challenge. Trust me, losing a key to a hardened steel lock is an inconvenience that is best to avoid is at all possible.

The first and foremost step you can take in organizing and managing your key inventory is to write down your key numbers and keep the list somewhere safe. This can be done on a computer, which is handy, but should be on paper somewhere as well. Remember, computers can crash and take your important information with them.

Beyond keeping your key numbers written down and safe, you need to keep your keys safe and organized as well. The best way to do this is with a key locker. These can be purchased very reasonably at an office supply store. With a key locker, all of your keys are kept in a central place. Additionally, each key can be numbered, labeled and sorted.

Following a simple key management plan will just eliminate a potential headache before it starts. Doing so will simply make your business more efficient and profitable and easier to operate.

Keeping Your Machines Looking Professional

This section is republished from Vending Machine Fundamentals in its entirety. Keeping your machines clean is always important and relevant.

Keeping your machines looking professional is an important responsibility. You need to make sure that your machines compliment the business locations where they reside. If your machines are dirty and unprofessional looking, they convey a bad message from you and the location and may upset business owners and customers alike.

Keeping your machines looking professional is really all about cleaning. To do this you need to keep a cleaning kit in your service vehicle. This kit should include:

- Glass cleaner
- All-purpose cleaner in a spray bottle
- Paper Towels
- Razor blade (good for graffiti)
- WD-40
- Q-tips
- Alcohol pads

Each time you service your machines, inspect them for grime or graffiti and make use of the cleaning kit as needed. Keep them looking as clean as possible.

Field Equipment

While the equipment needs of a bulk vending business are modest, you will need to make sure your business is outfitted with a few essentials.

A simple home tool set is an absolute must when you are in the field. Without a complete tool set, you will not be able to fix even the most basic of problems that occur with your machines. In the tool kit, make sure that you have the following at the very least:

- Hammer
- Pliers
- Wrench
- Ratchet Set
- Interchangeable screwdriver
- Screwdriver bits
- Pocket Knife
- Flashlight
- Needle nose pliers

This list of tools will see you through most of the repairs that you will encounter with your route. You can easily buy a simple to carry kit, like the one shown below at most general stores and home repair stores. Wherever you buy your tools, you should not need to spend more than $20 for the complete set.

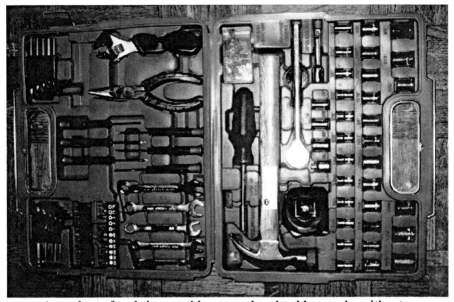
A good set of tools is something a vendor should never be without.

Refunds

Mechanical vending machines offer much greater reliability than their full service counterparts. They are much simpler systems, and by extension, they have fewer problems. All that being said, you still need to have a plan to issue refunds in the event of unsuccessful vends or if customers are unhappy with your product. This plan should be made very clear to the account manager as well once the machines are installed. The manager should never be left unsure of what to do and be forced to give refunds out of their own pocket.

How you deal with refunds is something for you to decide. You can drive out to every location in the event of a problem and personally hand someone a refund or proper product. You can be called and issue the refund by mail. Ultimately you just need to make sure that you have a plan and that everyone involved in the location is aware of it, especially the manager.

A Few Odds And Ends

The next sections, are useful pieces of information that you should know as a bulk vending operator. However, they don't really fit into any of the chapters already in this book. As such, they are thrown in here.

Keep Machines In Reserve

Sadly, sometimes your machines may be stolen or vandalized. Sometimes, machines will break severely enough to require you to remove them from the field and repair them in a workshop, or even professionally. When this happens, you will have a location without a machine. If the machine is not repaired quickly and correctly, you may loose an account and a source of income. It is possible that a long delay may not even be your fault. You may need to order a part that will take a few days to cross the country.

To combat this problem it is never a bad idea to have a few spare machines around. This works especially well with the small single and multiple select bulk machines. Whenever a need arises, you will have a reserve that can quickly be put into service to keep the account happy and keep earning you money.

This does not work with the more expensive machines however. It would be a bad business decision to go out a spend $500 on a new rack system to keep idle while you wait for another one to be vandalized.

Chance As A Marketing Tool

If you ever took the time to study the contents of capsule vending machines, a curious pattern would begin to emerge. In the case of a gumball vending machine, a customer knows that they will receive a gumball. However, often, in capsule machines, there is a variety of items that can be vended. This is in part a marketing tactic that you as a bulk vending operator should have a keen understanding of.

With multiple items available for sale in the machine, and no way to control which items are sold and when (other than their organization in the machine hopper) a customer may not receive the item that they wanted. In that case, they may choose to put more money into the machine in the hopes of receiving the originally sought after item. This increases sales and consequently the profits from the machine.

This can be expanded even more by placing an item of higher perceived value into a machine hopper with items that are of lower perceived value. For example, if you were selling jewelry through a capsule machine, you might look add an inexpensive watch to the display. This item has a higher perceived value than the other necklaces, bracelets and rings in the machine. Of course, the shown item needs to be in the machine or else you are being deceitful, but there does not need to be many of them. Then a customer might purchase several items hoping to get the watch. The item may be vended, or the customer may run out of money beforehand. However, again, you will have increased the number of sales, and you profits as well. This same tactic is often used by crane machine operators to increase their sales. By adding one really nice product into a machine, people will often spend more money by trying to retrieve it.

Emergency Fund

Any business would be well advised to maintain an emergency fund. This is no less true with a bulk vending machines route. The purpose of a fund like this can by manifold. It may be that there is a break in and one of your machines is stolen. Well to keep the account, you may have to go and buy a new machine that day. Your entire inventory may be lost to poor storage conditions. If this happens, you will need money to quickly replace your supplies. The reasons may not even be bad. You may suddenly be presented by a new and promising business opportunity. In order to take advantage of this, you may need to make a quick investment. You could rely on credit, but it is always a sound financial decision to swear off credit and grow with only wholly owned resource such as savings.

Building an emergency fund may not be possible as soon as you start operations. However, you can build one over time with the revenues from your machines. One common method of saving is to simply take a percentage of your revenue and lock it away in an account.

10% is a good place to start and should not be an undue burden on your new enterprise.

You also will need to give some thought to where you keep your emergency fund. Ideally, this money would receive a competitive rate of interest while remaining easily accessible to you should the need arise. A money market fund is a common bank account type that offers a slightly higher amount of interest while keeping you money available in cash. In many cases, you can even write checks from these accounts. Any bank will offer these accounts, but search around because rates vary quite a bit. One great resource when seeking higher rates of interest is Bankrate.com (www.bankrate.com). On this website, you can shop the rates of many different financial institutions to find the one that will best suit your particular needs.

No matter where you choose to keep your emergency fund, make sure that you treat it according and use it only for emergencies. This account should both be used to pay for personal expenses or the day to day operations of the vending business.

Conclusion

Once you have your machines in place, your route is ready to go and really will require very little maintenance. Service it regularly and collect the money. Make sure you maintain a good relationship with the business owners and managers that you work with, and make sure to run your route professionally. Keep your machines clean and looking professional. If you follow these few basics steps, there is no reason that the bulk route that you build cannot continue to generate large returns on your investment for years to come. Good luck!

Check Out These Other Great Titles From Pratzen Publishing

Vending Machine Fundamentals: How To Build Your Own Route

by Steven Woodbine

This book is a complete guide to building your own full service vending business based on soda and snack machines. This book walks you through goals, financing, corporate structure, vending business models, maintenance, service vehicles, inventory management, business analysis, and writing a business plan.

$14.95

Vending Machine Fundamentals Volume II: Success Strategies For Building Your Own Bulk Route

By Steven Woodbine

This is the second volume in the Vending Machine Fundamentals series. This book explains in simple English how to build and manage your own bulk vending business. This books covers who a bulk vending business is right for, various machine types, product lines, inventory management and the specific particulars of managing a bulk vending route.

$14.95

Making Money With Storage Auctions

By Edward Busoni

It is not common knowledge that every day across America, hundreds of storage lockers are auctioned off to winning bidders. The property in these units is often sold at tiny fractions of what the goods are actually worth. Inside this book, the author explains how you can start and profit from a storage auction business. Best of all a business of this type can be started for almost nothing!

$14.95

Fundamentals Of Offshore Banking: How To Open Accounts Almost Anywhere

By Walter Tyndale

This book explores the global banking industry. Inside the covers you will find information on why you might want to open an account in a foreign country, how to do so, and advice on how to protect your deposit. Additionally, many of the countries that will accept foreign deposits are profiled with information about banking regulators and institutions.

$14.95

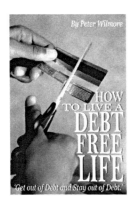

How To Live A Debt Free Life: Get Out Of Debt And Stay Out Of Debt

By Peter Wilmore

Learn how to free yourself from debt forever inside the pages of this book. The author of this book overcame his own debt and explains how through common sense and careful money management, you can too. In addition, there are chapters about starting to invest for retirement and how to protect yourself and family with insurance.

$9.95

Bartending Basics: A Complete Beginner's Guide

By Thomas Morrell

This book is a how-to guide written by ten year veteran of the restaurant and bar industry. Inside you will learn all about beer, wine and distilled spirits, as well as bartending techniques, ways to remember recipes, responsible bartending, cost and crowd control. There is also a chapter about how to put together a resume and how to find a job to start your new career.

$14.95